LOSING MY BROTHER

A YOUNGER BROTHER'S MEMOIR OF SUICIDE

by Robert Henslin

AFTER THE FIRE PRESS

REDDING, CALIFORNIA

If you or someone you love is in crisis, contact the
American Foundation for Suicide Prevention.

OR TEXT **TALK** TO **741741**

Losing My Brother

Copyright © 2023 Robert Henslin. All rights reserved.

This book is non-fiction. All dates and events, persons, dialogue and description of locales and places are as accurate as possible, based on the recollections and impressions of the author. In some instances, personal names have been changed out of respect for their privacy. Product or service brands referenced in this work are the property of their respective companies.

The material presented in this book is for information purposes only, and is not intended as a substitute for professional medical advice. Individuals with medical questions or conditions are advised to consult their physician.

No part of this book may be reproduced in any form or by any electronic or mechanical means including information storage and retrieval systems, without permission in writing from the author. The only exception is by a reviewer, who may quote short excerpts in a review.

Scripture taken from the New King James Version®. Copyright © 1982 by Thomas Nelson. Used by permission. All rights reserved.

Published in the United States by After the Fire Press and Kindle Direct Publishing, an Amazon.com company. First Edition.

Printed in the United States of America.

Book cover design by Robert Henslin

Page layout by Rich Bullock www.perilousfiction.com

ISBN #978-0-9853736-5-8

Losing My Brother is available at Amazon.com.

V 08/8/23

CONTENTS

Preface ix

1. Breaking the Seal — 1
2. An Ominous Message — 5
3. Next of Kin — 13
4. Frazzled — 15
5. The First Hump — 19
6. Diving in Deep — 29
7. Cleaning, Sorting and Feral Cats — 33
8. On the Treadmill — 39
9. Looking Back — 43
10. Wanderings — 55
11. Trying To Make Sense of It All — 61
12. Lament — 71
13. Realizations — 75
14. An Exercise of Lament — 79
15. Final Thoughts — 89

Appendix — 91
Notes — 111
Bibliography — 113
Resources — 115
Acknowledgments — 119
About the Author — 121
Also by Robert Henslin — 123

*To my friend, the late Cory Severud,
who convinced me to finish writing this book.
May you rest in peace among the angels.*

PREFACE

When the thought of writing this memoir first crossed my mind, I immediately dismissed it. At that time, only a year had passed since my brother's death in the late summer of 2016. I was still wrapping up chores in my role as executor of his estate. When not distracted by that work I was trying to maintain my sanity—mentally, emotionally and spiritually.

But like hummingbirds swarming a bowl of sugar water, thoughts about writing this book continued to pester me. *Not now. It's just not the time,* I repeatedly told myself. But at some point, rather than dismiss those thoughts outright, I decided to let them come and go, trusting God would bring a sense of peace about undertaking such a project if it was meant to be.

That peace didn't come until the spring of 2021.

A few days after celebrating my 59th birthday in late March, I leaned into that peace and, as my schedule allowed, began roughing out the first inklings of a story arc for the new book. Emotions ran high at times, as the reality that I was trying to craft a story about my own brother's death was ever-present. Not too far into the work, I realized whatever it was I was trying to put together would take considerable energy, intestinal fortitude and time.

Preface

But I hadn't a clue about just how much of those precious commodities would be required.

On an otherwise wonderful spring day in early April of '21, a strange feeling came over me. I couldn't see anything in the upper left corner of my field of vision. And though my thinking was clear, very little of what I said out loud made any sense.

Uh, oh. Stroke? Something.

After several hours in my local hospital's Emergency Room, the doctors determined I had experienced a "pre-migraine event"—no headache, just some of the fun stuff that can happen if a headache may be looming on the horizon.

The same thing happened a couple weeks later, but on that occasion, I had to abandon my fully loaded shopping cart in a grocery store when my right leg decided it had other plans and took on a life of its own. After a second day-long stay in the ER, a brain scan confirmed the presence of a (thankfully) benign Meningioma tumor in my left parietal lobe.

A what?

I had already spent a quarter of my life dealing with significant medical issues, but these were uncharted waters. Yet again, I had to shift my mental gears into "medical" mode, this time working with both a neurologist and brain surgeon to determine the best course of treatment.

My doctors advised a "watch and wait" approach to the tumor. When first discovered, it was quite small and could be monitored with brain imaging as needed. Armed only with meds designed to suppress pre-migraine symptoms, daily life became rather tentative.

I had my meds and groceries delivered rather than risk a second "cart abandonment" scenario—or worse. My friends checked in with me each day to ensure I wasn't crumpled up in a corner, rambling on about how cool it would be to have a unicorn for a pet.

Book? What book?

Preface

After four months of trying hard not to live dangerously, a scheduled brain MRI indicated the tumor had doubled in size.

Next stop for the crazy train—brain surgery.

A craniotomy was performed in late September of 2021, and with great success. Three days in the hospital allowed the anesthesia to work its way out of my system. I spent much of my time arguing with the drawstrings on my hospital gown and trying to figure out how to operate the TV remote.

Nine days in a rehab hospital followed. Beyond several hours of physical and occupational therapy sessions each day, helping the staff hang Halloween decorations all over the unit was an integral part of my daily routine. After returning home, I was overwhelmed with joy. I had survived brain surgery, rehab, way too much hospital jello and was excited about getting back to work on this book.

I felt blessed to be alive.

Follow-up brain MRIs were performed every three months to monitor the healing of the surgical site and check for new tumor growth. My marching orders were clear—live as full a life as was possible. With God's grace, the manuscript became a living, breathing entity—perhaps more vibrant and alive at the time than me.

But an MRI in late August of 2022 confirmed the presence of a new tumor growing in at essentially the same spot as the first. Rather than a second brain surgery, a six-week course of daily brain radiation (with weekends off for good behavior) was prescribed, in hopes the size of the tumor could be significantly reduced. I was able to drive myself to the appointments, but on several of those 10-minute treks, thoughts that perhaps I was *not* supposed to write this book crossed what remained of my mind.

Thankfully, the six weeks seemed to fly by. The radiation treatment concluded just four days before Christmas in 2022. As the New Year kicked off, work on this book ramped up once again. By mid-April, the manuscript was finished and ready for the refining fire of the editing process.

Preface

I had peace when I began this writing journey, and still do. If sharing my suicide story helps even a single person, enduring the rollercoaster ride to get it published will have been well worth it.

"It is not what a man does that is of final importance, but what he is in what he does. The atmosphere produced by a man, much more than his abilities, has the lasting influence."

– Oswald Chambers
from *Baffled to Fight Better –
Job and the Problem of Suffering*

Losing My Brother

A younger brother's memoir of suicide

1

BREAKING THE SEAL

Sixteen concrete steps led us up to the front entrance of the old Victorian home. I located the key left for me under one of the two planters flanking each side of the door. At some point in history this three-story home was converted into six apartments, with two units per floor. The door to Unit 201 was immediately to our left as we entered the building.

I stood for a moment with my good friend Gordon in the stillness of the small lobby, staring at the unit's heavy metal door. It was sealed to the jam with a large, square adhesive label, folded in an "L." During a painful phone conversation four days prior, I was told I would find such a label.

In my left hand I held a tarnished brass key to the apartment, that for many years had been tucked away in a desk drawer in my office. I fidgeted nervously with it while Gordon waited patiently behind me. I reached up and dragged it through the label, leaving a jagged trail of torn stickiness in its wake.

"Are you ready for this?" Gordon asked.

"No, man," I replied. "Not at all."

I was anywhere else but there.

Though we were unsure of what we would encounter on the

other side of the door, we knew full well we had to face this first, terrible step.

The deadbolt slid open easily. With a slight push on the door to persuade it over a worn metal threshold, Gordon and I entered the apartment. We paused for a moment in the middle of the living room and glanced up at the plaster ceiling twelve feet overhead. The air was thick with a ripe, stinging sweetness that to this day is difficult to forget.

Almost instantly, Gordon and I felt uneasy and sensed an oppressive presence. What had been a space warmed by family, friends and festive celebrations for nearly two decades, felt like a tomb drained of all life and all good things. Light, it seemed, was consumed by darkness.

At one end of the room, tall drapes drawn closed in front of a large bay window discouraged views of the neighborhood and street scene below. At the far end, a darkened alcove shared a wall with a short hallway that accessed a modest bathroom and the only bedroom.

Gordon and I felt the need to pray before we did anything else. We prayed through each part of the 620 square foot unit.

We prayed in Jesus' name and declared evil had no authority and no claim on this space. I had only prayed that type of prayer one other time in my life when the sense of evil matched what I felt in this apartment.

When we concluded, the oppression that seemed to smother the place was gone. Neither of us felt especially happy but the eye contact we exchanged, at that moment, spoke volumes about the relief we both felt.

Again, we moved through each room, this time to gain a sense of the scope of work that lay before us. Stacks of paperwork covered a glass-topped coffee table in the living room, along with some loose change, bank statements and a checkbook.

In the tiny kitchen, a faintly humming refrigerator chilled plastic containers full of leftovers, half-empty bottles of salad dressing, and an open box of baking soda. At the end of a long, narrow counter, a red light flashed atop a phone message machine indicating 30 unplayed messages.

As our walk-thru continued, I felt awkward...almost like a burglar who invaded someone's home. *This isn't my stuff. What am I doing here? I am not supposed to be here now.* My uneasiness grew as Gordon and I moved down the short hallway, past the bathroom where a single toothbrush rested in a cup next to a bottle of cologne on the counter.

As we approached the bedroom at the end of the hall, I had a golf ball-sized lump in my throat. I followed my friend through the doorway. It was the only room in the apartment I had not fully entered when we prayed a few moments earlier.

I wanted nothing to do with this room.

We stopped at the foot of a double bed that was flanked on each side by two wall-mounted lighting sconces. On an outside wall next to the bed, brown linen curtains nearly obscured a large double-hung window. A faded, filtered glow from the mid-afternoon sun was the only light that pierced the otherwise darkened space.

Thin ribbons of light reached across the top of the bed. There was something odd about the way the fitted sheet was stretched over the mattress. It took a moment for our eyes to adjust and realize what we were seeing.

A six-foot long almond shaped section of material nearly two feet wide had been cut out and removed from the center of the fitted sheet. It was then the full weight of what transpired in this place two weeks prior washed over me.

My big brother—my only brother—was dead. He took his own life. He was gone.

2

AN OMINOUS MESSAGE

It had been another typical late August day in Cottonwood, California. Daytime high temperatures, that time of year in the North State, could reach the 100-degree mark without even trying. In the evening, the heat was often tempered by a cool breeze that picked up around sundown. By midnight, a 40-degree difference could separate the day's high and low temperatures.

On that cool, quiet Wednesday evening, I was hanging out with two good friends, watching TV and recounting the day's events. Tony and Judy had known me and my family for more than fifty years. I was renting a room in their home, and at that point in time, had lived with them for four and a half years. There was a comfortable vibe among us. We shared a very deep friendship and had been there for each other through many highs and lows over the years.

At about 8:30 p.m. that evening, a new text message brought my mobile phone to life.

"Rob, This is Gary. I'm a neighbor of your brother. I live in one of the other units. No one has seen Bill for a couple weeks. So we are all concerned. He listed you as his emergency contact, so I'm reaching out."

I read the message to Tony and Judy, then replied to Gary, thanking him for contacting me and assuring him I would take immediate action.

A dozen or more rings had me anxious when I called my brother. *Come on, man. Pick up.* When I was about to end the call, his recorded greeting kicked in.

"Hi, this is Bill. Please leave a message and I'll call you back."

I was unsure how much time I'd have for my message.

"Hey, Bill. I just received a concerning text message from your neighbor Gary. No one has seen you around or heard from you in a couple weeks. I'm concerned about you, bro. If I don't hear from you in the next five minutes, I'm going to call the San Francisco Police and request a welfare check. I hope you're okay. Please call me."

I never wanted anything more in my life than to hear my brother's voice.

As I reengaged with Tony and Judy, our now tentative conversation entertained possible explanations for Bill's falling off the radar. *Maybe he got hit with a summer bug and has been sick in bed. Perhaps he decided to jet over to Hawaii.* He had done that on several occasions in the past.

My mind wandered as the three of us talked. I tried to recall my last conversation with Bill. His 58th birthday had just past. I had left a greeting for him when I called on his big day—August 24th. He hadn't returned my call.

At the time, that didn't strike me as odd, as Bill and I played a lot of phone tag over the years. In more recent history, the frequency of our interactions had dropped off considerably. I knew he liked to screen his calls and, for the most part, didn't enjoy long phone chats—unless *he* had something to discuss.

When five minutes had passed I dialed up the San Francisco Police Department and requested the welfare check. After providing the dispatcher with Bill's address and phone number, I asked if my request was considered a high priority. I was told it was a very busy night but that an officer would be dispatched to the address as soon as possible.

The waiting game began.

After ending the call, a random realization came to mind—I had a key to Bill's apartment, but not for the main entrance to the building. And I had only been inside his place one time many years earlier, when Bill hosted our family for Christmas dinner.

Thankfully, a year prior, I had mentioned to him that if something were to happen, I had no idea what his wishes were regarding a burial, memorial service or what he wanted done with all his stuff. Bill's reaction had been one of surprise coupled with appreciation for my bringing the matter up. Within a couple weeks, I received his completed Last Will and Testament via Certified Mail.

I returned to the company of Tony and Judy, and we continued our speculation about what might have happened to Bill. Over the previous several weeks, the three of us had wondered about the possibility he might decide he was done dealing with personal challenges that had been eating away at him for a number of years.

We had talked that day about it, as it had been some time since I had heard a word from my brother. As difficult as this is to admit, a part of me quietly gave up hope the police would find Bill safe and sound. It hurts to high heaven to even type these words.

How could I quit on my brother so easily?

As I waited for word about Bill, I thought about our history and the challenges and curveballs we encountered in our lives. I considered how we had each chosen to respond to them and how those events had impacted us. We had talked a lot, shared insights and opinions, thought through perplexing situations and quite often joked with each other and laughed a bunch along the way.

After many of our conversations, I felt upbeat and encouraged, but rarely felt I had been able to do the same for Bill.

One major event happened in 2009, when I received a bone marrow transplant following a relapse of blood cancer after a nearly 20-year long first remission. Complications and side effects of the treatment had kept me tap dancing through minefields ever since.

Then, my marriage of 22 years ended in a horribly draining divorce in 2012. I was working only part time as physical exhaustion and a run to the local hospital Emergency Room was never more than a heartbeat away.

Over the years life had gnawed away at my brother as well. After completing his college studies in engineering, Bill determined that field wasn't a good fit. He pursued other avenues for a time, but after several years decided to move to Washington State for a change of scenery, a new perspective and in time, a job as a technical writer and editor at a thriving technology company he was excited about.

Nearly a decade later, what he had described to me as "a pressure cooker" work environment—where his fellow employees logged 80-hour weeks and crashed in sleeping bags stowed under their desks—had sucked the life out of him. Too much time there had led to disillusionment and burnout. That, coupled with an overabundance of the rain, snow and iced

An Ominous Message

lattes of the Pacific Northwest pretty much drove Bill to the edge.

"I think I've just had it with life up here," he said during a phone conversation.

At that time, he had retired from the work force to clear his head and was in the midst of a long-term restoration of his 1950s bungalow-style home. I had been under the impression he was enjoying the process.

"How 'had it' are you?" I asked. "Enough to move?"

"I don't know," he responded. "Three weeks ago I applied oil-based paint to the window trim on the outside of the house and it's still wet. The air temperature hasn't been above 37 degrees for a couple weeks and all the new paint is covered with tiny beads of water."

From that point on there seemed to be a growing frustration quietly churning inside my brother. He rarely mentioned the bungalow—until he sold the place in 1997. Once he closed escrow, Bill moved to San Francisco and, for the first time in quite a while, seemed really happy.

Twelve years later in 2009, the stock market crashed. When the dust settled, it seemed Bill's world had become much smaller. He did less traveling—perhaps less living—than he had done previously. He didn't like to drive anywhere if he could avoid it and often commented about needing to keep a lid on his expenses.

But in 2010, my brother's life was impacted even more dramatically—in a matter of just a few seconds.

As he was leaving a favorite restaurant in San Francisco, Bill was jumped, robbed and left nearly unconscious in some bushes outside a parking garage. Other patrons of the restaurant found him and called 911. His wallet had been stolen, and just twenty minutes after the attack, security cameras at a nearby drug store recorded his assailant trying to make a purchase using one of Bill's credit cards.

I received a call a couple hours later from a social worker at

San Francisco General Hospital, alerting me they had Bill in the ER and that I would need to come get him. He had received a significant blow to the head, was exhibiting signs of a concussion and would need to be watched through the night.

My phone number was the only one Bill could remember.

Finding my brother on one of a dozen gurneys lining the hallway of the Emergency department, and seeing the abrasions, bruises and patches of dried blood about his head and face shook me up.

I wanted five minutes with the guy who jumped him.

Bill asked me what happened and why he was in the hospital. I told him he had been attacked and robbed. He nodded. "Oh, that's right." I told him I was there to take him back to my place. About 30 seconds later, he looked up at me from the gurney with a surprised look on his face.

"Rob, what are *you* doing here?"

In the years following the attack, Bill's outlook seemed to take a dramatic, downward turn. His frustrations about the trajectory of his career and a growing discontentment with life in San Francisco became more and more pronounced. He often commented that the vibe of the city had changed since he had first moved there—and not for the better.

"People are different now," he stated on more than one occasion. "Everyone has their Bluetooth devices sticking out of their ears. They talk out loud as they walk down the street, but no one even says, 'hi' anymore."

And though he lived in a beautiful part of California, the cold weather and fog clouded his ability to enjoy the many days each year where San Francisco's blue sky, sunshine and fresh air were breathtaking.

I was frustrated for him—and *by* him—but tried to be supportive.

Beyond our individual challenges, Bill and I shared joint Power of Attorney responsibilities for our parents. They had set up a Family Trust that spelled out in no uncertain terms our duties and responsibilities as co-trustees.

Our dad had passed away in 1999 (just three months short of his 93rd birthday). Mom was twenty years younger than Dad and, after his passing, purposed to live as full a life as possible and enjoy every minute—and she had a blast. But by the time Mom was in her early eighties, her physical and mental decline began to manifest and accelerate.

Bill and I held dramatically different positions regarding the medical establishment. He loathed "Big Pharma." I had way too much experience with medications I knew had benefitted me immensely.

By God's grace, my brother had never been gravely ill and forced to entrust his life to a team of medical specialists. I had spent a quarter of my life doing precisely that.

My brother was suspicious of most doctors. I had received excellent care from my doctors and believed every one of my nurses were Heaven-sent, under-appreciated angels.

Such deeply divergent perspectives provided a seedbed for an ongoing wrestling match over how best to address numerous issues related to our mom's advancing age, including the onset of Alzheimer's disease and Mom's ever-increasing need for greater levels of care.

Our philosophical head banging placed our relationship under significant strain for the better part of a decade.

As I reflected on that history and awaited word about Bill, a part of me acknowledged the possibility he had grown so tired of life's challenges and stressors, that he decided to draw a line in the sand and end his life.

I struggled in the moment to know what to do with that thought, and still do.

My conversation with Tony and Judy was interrupted by the ringing of my phone. An hour had passed since I had spoken with the police dispatcher. There was no caller ID accompanying the number, but I recognized the "415" area code as coming from the San Francisco Bay Area. I was greeted by a female voice with a soothing Irish accent.

"Rob, this is Janine. I'm a friend and neighbor of your dear brother, Bill."

"Oh, yes. Thank you for calling."

"Listen, Rob, I'm here with the Police."

I hung on every word Janine uttered. *Where was this going?*

"We're outside your brother's apartment."

"Oh, I called the police and asked for a welfare check about an hour ago."

"Yes, dear. Now there is a terrible smell coming from Bill's unit..."

A terrible smell...

I don't recall much else Janine said after hearing those words. *Gut punch.* Tears I had been holding back welled up in my eyes. I fought to hold it together as I strained to catch Janine's final words.

"The police are asking me to return to my apartment. I'll try to update you a bit later, dear."

I believe I thanked Janine but honestly don't remember. When the call ended, I turned to Tony and Judy and lost it.

"That was another of Bill's neighbors," I stammered. "The police are there and there's a really bad smell coming from Bill's apartment."

When I uttered those words, Tony lowered his head for a moment; a former paramedic with the Los Angeles City Fire Department, he knew full well what that meant.

In just a split second, it felt like hope had been swept away by the evening breeze. A somber mood fell over the conversation in the living room like a wet blanket smothering a campfire.

Was this really happening?

3

NEXT OF KIN

"Is this Robert Henslin?" The man's voice was confident, yet cautious.

"Yes, it is."

"Is your brother William Henslin, Jr.?"

"Uh, yes."

There was a brief pause.

"Robert, I'm with the San Francisco County Coroner's office. I have some difficult news to relay to you."

At 11:59 p.m. on August 31, 2016, I received official notice that my brother was dead.

While I sat at a counter in the kitchen, tracing grout lines in the tile surface with my finger, the Coroner's investigator detailed the events of the past several hours. Firemen had gained access to the apartment through a balcony and pair of narrow French doors off the unit's kitchen. Bill's body was found on his bed in the bedroom.

I had waited for a call I hoped with everything in me would not bring terrible news. It was only God's grace that allowed me to be present enough mentally to focus on what the man from the Coroner's office was saying.

"I can't speculate on the exact cause of death," he said, "but I can tell you bottles of over-the-counter sleep aids and pain relievers were found on a nightstand next to the bed."

Oh, Lord. Here it comes.

"What appears to be a handwritten 'note of intent' was left on a table in the front room."

"How long do you think the body had been there," I asked.

"Three to ten days based on what I found at the scene."

My mind went blank. For a second time, a pause halted our conversation.

"I know this is very difficult, Robert," the man said. "I gathered up a wallet containing a driver's license and credit cards, along with a set of keys, what appeared to be a Last Will and Testament and the note of intent," he explained. "Those items will be in an envelope you can pick up at our Bryant Street offices downtown."

I thanked the man and apologized for my frazzled state.

Before ending the call, the man told me an autopsy would need to be performed to determine the exact cause of death, and also that for security purposes, he had placed an official seal—a large sticker, about the size of my hand—that secured Bill's apartment door to the jam. I was the only one authorized to break the seal and enter the property.

Though it felt like an hour, our conversation had lasted just a few minutes. When the call ended, I was spent. My brother was dead and he might have taken his own life.

Hadn't I just talked with him a few days ago?

4

FRAZZLED

On the night I learned of Bill's passing, I spent seven hours staring at the spinning ceiling fan in my room, unable to turn off a constant stream of thoughts.

Over and over I replayed the events of the evening, like a super fan reviewing the plays of the week. *Nobody had seen Bill for nearly two weeks. Firemen found his body in his bedroom. He may have committed suicide. He left a note. What did it say? He was only 58 years old.*

During breakfast the next morning, my brain was nowhere to be found. Thankfully, Tony's was still present and working.

"You know, Rob, today is September 1st," he said.

The significance of that fact was lost on me. Tony continued.

"What are the odds your brother's mortgage payment is due today?"

Reality check.

"You could call the mortgage company and ask," Tony suggested.

I retreated to my room and fumbled around for a time, trying to locate the mortgage company's contact information. It was somewhere. I was elsewhere.

As I placed the call, I wondered if I should mention Bill's

passing. "Good morning," I started. "My brother just had a birthday and I'd like to pay this month's mortgage payment for him."

Both of those statements were true.

"Well, aren't you a good brother," the woman responded.

"Is the payment due today?" I asked.

"It is. But there's a ten-day grace period."

I cut a check after ending the call. Mission accomplished.

For the balance of the day, I dove in as best I could in an effort to wrap my head around the myriad tasks now looming on the horizon. As I read and reread the original copy of Bill's Last Will and Testament, it didn't take long to realize I was in for quite a ride—in territory where I had very limited experience.

My divorce four years prior had been a trial-by-fire introduction to the inner workings of the legal system, in spite of growing up hearing numerous descriptions of legal discourse from my dad, who never lost a case in fifty years of medical malpractice defense litigation. Bill had drawn up a Last Will and Testament document but didn't have a Trust in place to prevent his estate from going into Probate upon his death. Some online research alerted me to the coming paper chase.

An official court case would be established to determine the authenticity and validity of my brother's Will. Such cases could remain open a year or more, depending on the complexity of the estate. A long list of questions would have to be answered.

Was the Last Will and Testament document valid?

Who were the heirs and beneficiaries of the decedent, if any?

Did the decedent own any property of significant value?

Had the decedent left any outstanding debts?

What was the decedent's shoe size?

Did the decedent prefer paper bags or plastic?

Did the decedent enjoy walks on the beach or not so much?

Ugh.

Rather than a funeral or graveside service, Bill had indicated in his Will his preference for a direct burial in a simple pine box.

That eliminated the need for many costly mortuary services. His wish was to be quietly laid to rest in the same cemetery where our dad had been buried in 1999.

I spent time that day engaged in awkward phone conversations with folks from the cemetery and mortuary, both located four hours south of Cottonwood near San Jose, California.

The man from the mortuary initiated the paperwork for a direct burial and emailed me the full list of charges for their services. When I mentioned the requirement of an autopsy, the man assured me he would contact the Coroner's office that afternoon, and thought it quite possible his office could take possession of Bill's body within one to two weeks.

I thanked the man for his time, but still wondered what impact the autopsy might have on Bill's request for a simple, direct burial. In a conversation that afternoon with a clerk at the Coroner's office in San Francisco, I learned their facility alone handled all autopsies for a tri-county area—a landmass with a population in excess of 4.4 million people. Around 1400 autopsies were performed at that office each year.

Great.

The clerk described their backlog as "significant." Rather than the two weeks estimated for completion of the autopsy, I figured a more realistic timeframe would be closer to several months.

Beyond establishing a basic framework for interment of Bill's body and securing a burial plot near our dad, it seemed that portion of my work as executor of my brother's estate was at a standstill until an official cause of death had been determined.

By nightfall, I was exhausted. As I prepared for bed, a strange realization came to mind—I hadn't shed a tear all day.

I had thought of my brother countless times. I stared at his handwriting on official forms and pieces of correspondence. I laughed out loud over the ridiculous tail-chase probate was going to be as I read about it online. I even spent hours on the phone, talking with perfect strangers about Bill's death and his final wishes.

But I felt completely void of emotion—numb, I suppose, in the truest sense of the word.

I killed the light in my room around 9:30 p.m. As I had done the night before, I stared at the ceiling fan with my mind in hyper drive, thinking about the list of names I would need to put together to inform family and friends of Bill's passing, the need to find an attorney to walk me through probate, the need to schedule the first trip to Bill's apartment and on and on.

There were too many tasks stacking up, like a line of jets holding for takeoff at the end of a runway. But in the midst of that mess, there was never a single moment of reflection over the personal tragedy that had befallen me just 24 hours earlier.

Didn't I care?

5

THE FIRST HUMP

As I drove away from Tony and Judy's place, I wondered if my timing was right. It had been three days since I'd received word of Bill's passing. *Was it too soon to make the four-hour trek to his apartment? Perhaps I should have stuck around longer and checked off more items on the mother of all "to-do" lists.*

Those were my only thoughts as I ventured out on Day 1 of a planned four-day trip. I certainly wasn't eager to go. But I was eager to get over the first hump—whatever that meant, whatever it needed to look like and however it needed to play out.

I had only the knowledge my brother was dead, but little else. The names of two of Bill's neighbors, a vague sense of the timeline of events surrounding his passing, and only a sketchy awareness that life would never be the same, was all I carried with me.

An hour into my dance with the interstate traffic, I realized I was cruising along in total silence. Typically, the radio would have been blasting and I would have been singing along (terribly but enthusiastically) to whatever was tuned in. Not so much this time. I hadn't a thought about the radio, or much else after the ten-minute drive from Tony's place to the interstate on-ramp.

I'd made trips up and down Interstate 5 on multiple

occasions. It is one of the main arteries connecting the northern, central and southern regions of the state. The scenery is a mix of agriculture and rolling ranch land, old and new residential and commercial developments and, every now and then, some full-blown urban infrastructure.

I-5 isn't a straight line, but as the hours stacked up, it could begin to feel that way.

There are a few favorite places along that highway where I liked to stop for a stretch. Roberta's Taqueria in Williams makes the best Carnitas burritos in the North State (in my humble opinion). Nearby Granzella's Market and Restaurant was a favorite stop for my family when my two daughters were young, and we'd spend portions of their summer vacations on multi-family camping trips all over the state.

Granzella's is famous for a huge glass case containing two formerly very alive, 12-foot tall polar bears that greet thirsty travelers as they enter the bar and dining room.

As I passed the exit for those places, I thought about calling Bill. I knew he would crack up talking about stuffed polar bears and other roadside kitsch. We loved laughing about that kind of stuff.

Then a sobering realization came to mind—I couldn't call him. And I'd never again hear his voice.

Though the ultimate destination was Bill's apartment in San Francisco, the first leg of the journey was to the Sacramento Airport to pick up my best friend, Gordon. Good friends since our high school days, we had shared many great times together over the decades.

We had also been there for each other through some of life's most difficult circumstances. When I initially contacted Gordon to let him know what happened, his first words were, "What do you need me to do?"

The First Hump

The airport was two and a half hours south of Cottonwood. For much of the trip, I had been content with watching the scenery roll by, mile after mile. Then, kind of out of nowhere, thoughts about my faith and the difficult times I had endured over the years came to mind.

I'm a Christian whose spiritual birthday dates back to 1971. I was nine years old and part of a group of boys from my Sunday school class on a weekend camp out at Green Oak Ranch in Vista, California. After hearing a story about God being like a shepherd who loved and cared for his sheep, I made a campfire vespers decision to invite Jesus into my heart.

As the years passed, Sunday school was where I learned more about God, the Bible, the life of Jesus and what it meant to live out my faith each day. But my core beliefs—the foundations of my faith—weren't really challenged when I was a young boy.

However, when life got beyond real in my adult years and took several dramatic turns I hadn't seen coming, the impact of those events was soul crushing. Two battles with blood cancer, a bone marrow transplant and a divorce had slammed me hard over the previous 27 years and tested my faith to its core. In each case, only God knew how difficult and treacherous the road would be.

On several deeply reflective occasions during those storms, I questioned what I really believed. But at the end of those mental and spiritual gymnastics, what had always remained consistent was a simple faith that God was who his word said he was, and with that a sense of peace—in the midst of those troubles and in spite of not knowing how my circumstances would play out.

It wasn't a peace I created on my own—far from it. In the "self-made" category, I'm only proficient at impatience, overthinking, worry and the occasional loaf of fresh-baked banana bread.

Over the years, I experienced God's grace to endure my trials, his love, provision, and his miracles (ask me about my two daughters the medical establishment explained wouldn't be possible due to the ravages of chemotherapy).

In my mind, Jesus was the Son of God—born, lived, crucified and resurrected—and Savior of the world—or he was the biggest fraud ever perpetrated. As a young boy, I chose to believe the former assertion with simple faith. As I grew older and, frankly, cared more about my spiritual life, I prayed for a sharp mind and a teachable, moldable spirit, as neither of those qualities came naturally.

And I wasn't alone in my faith.

Bill and I grew up attending a Baptist church just a few minutes across town from our home in southern California. Our family had ties to the church that dated back many decades. My brother became a Christian there in 1965, when he was just seven years old.

About the time I became a teenager, I began seeing my big brother in a new way. We were different people, but very close. As I fumbled along with my faith in high school, Bill started college, and his faith seemed to deepen.

I never heard him spout a lot of "Jesus" talk. Instead, he was real—an authentic believer who walked the walk and sought the Lord. He seemed to genuinely trust that God loved us, knew us intimately, had a plan for our lives and walked with us through good times and bad.

One year during his undergraduate studies at Cal Tech, Bill led the Christian fellowship group on campus. I really admired him and the person he was becoming.

When I encountered life's curveballs, Bill was always an awesome brother. Though he lived in Washington State, he flew down to Southern California to be with me when I was diagnosed with leukemia in the fall of 1989.

Bill had his limits when it came to medical matters, but that didn't keep him from being a huge source of encouragement when the cancer returned 20 years later, and I received a bone marrow transplant in 2009.

And when my marriage of 22 years crashed and burned in 2012, Bill lent an encouraging ear whenever we talked—and never once uttered a disparaging word about his former sister-in-law.

With the Sacramento airport coming into view, I appreciated for the first time in a long while the rich history of brotherhood, faith and friendship Bill and I had shared. That brought a sense of comfort, but with it a realization that spiritually I felt as dead as a box of rocks.

My brother was dead. He may have killed himself. How could he have done that? Lots of folks loved him and cared about him. He knew that, didn't he? Could I have done something before everything went south? Did Bill just toss his faith out the window?

I had no peace.

I exited the interstate with that machine-gun-like barrage of thoughts firing in my head, but tried not to dwell on them. I figured they probably just needed to be left to simmer awhile. Pulling into the cell phone waiting area just inside the airport entrance, I longed for just one more conversation with Bill—to say I was sorry and say goodbye.

With the miles between us, Gordon and I didn't get to enjoy much time together. Parked in the airport's cell phone waiting area, it was great to receive his call and know he had arrived and his plane was taxiing to the gate. When I found him waiting outside the terminal a few minutes later, we greeted each other warmly and also acknowledged the terrible circumstances that brought us together.

Over the 38-year friendship Gordon and I had enjoyed, He and Bill developed their own friendship. "When you called me and broke the news, I was shocked," Gordon shared. "Bill is the first close person I've known who took their own life."

It was virgin territory for both of us.

The second leg of the journey took about an hour and a half. We knew very little about what we would find when we arrived at Bill's apartment. I had brought along a tall stack of banker's boxes so we could pack up the important paperwork, but figured we would identify many other items as well that should be part of the "first wave" of our security sweep.

We entered the outskirts of San Francisco from the north and crossed the Golden Gate Bridge in the early afternoon, under blue skies. The 66-degree temperature was a welcomed change from the heat of the North State. Gordon and I had enjoyed some good conversation on the trip but our spirits were tempered by the heaviness of the task before us.

Our first stop was the Coroner's office downtown, adjacent to the Hall of Justice. From the southern end of the Bridge it was a fifteen-minute drive south and east through the city. We joined the frenetic pace of the pulsing traffic and a knot began to tighten in my stomach.

Under normal circumstances I enjoyed certain aspects of San Francisco but never relished driving there. In the past, there had been times when my then wife and I ventured into the City to enjoy a meal at a favorite Italian restaurant—Mona Lisa, on Columbus Avenue. It was always a great time—once we found parking.

On the day Gordon and I made our way through the City, parking, especially around the Hall of Justice, was scarce. Thankfully, we scored a spot just a couple of blocks from the Hall. After feeding the parking meter with what seemed like a lifetime savings of quarters, Gordon and I made our way to the main entrance on Bryant Street.

I stated my business to a court officer. He led us past a packed security screening area, down a long echoing hallway and through a pair of foreboding, thick glass and brushed metal doors that could have been used to secure the White House from an attack. The officer gestured to a second set of equally intimidating doors farther ahead at the end of an inclined walkway.

"That's where you gentlemen want to head," the officer stated.

If he only knew how much that wasn't where I wanted to head.

In a thousand lifetimes I could never have imagined that someday I would use my brother's name and "Coroner's Office" in the same sentence.

After I handed my identification to the clerk behind the tall front counter, she disappeared into an adjacent room. After just a few minutes she returned and handed me the small brown envelope the investigator had mentioned on the night he informed me of Bill's passing.

I took a brief look inside the envelope to be sure everything listed on the inventory was accounted for, but with a growing disdain for the cold and impersonal feeling of the place, made it quick.

Gordon and I exited the office and made our way back to the truck, hopeful the many quarters we had fed the hungry parking meter kept my windshield free of a love letter from the San Francisco Police. On that short walk, I was struck with the reality of what the folks in the Coroner's office dealt with each day.

Unlike other government offices, it wasn't about driver's license renewals, job placement, housing assistance, Social Security benefits or voter registration.

Sobering. Humbling.

With my truck idling in our parking space, Gordon and I engaged in a moment of melancholy, as we considered the accomplishment of our first goal of the day. But as we headed back into traffic, our thoughts turned to the reality that, in another 10 minutes, we would begin the most difficult of tasks at Bill's place in Pacific Heights.

The route through the city mapped out on my phone took us north and west for just a few miles. At about the halfway mark, we made a left and began a westward crawl down Pine Street in wall-to-wall traffic. Waiting at each of the nine stoplights heightened the tension already churning inside me.

When I turned onto Bill's street, parking—again—was an issue. I laughed tentatively as I attempted to fit my 16-foot long truck up the building's sloped (and narrow) eight-foot long driveway. After setting the parking break, I glanced over at Gordon. Both of us were pressed firmly against our seat backs, enjoying a breathtaking view of my truck's headliner, like astronauts ready for launch.

I knew my parking job was surely going to hack someone off—probably a tenant, I figured, with a tiny Smartcar or MINI.

We climbed out of the truck and met on the sidewalk. The mood turned more serious as we glanced up at the face of the vintage Victorian home. Immediately my eyes were drawn to the small Juliet-style balcony and the two, narrow French doors firemen had used to gain entry into Bill's apartment.

With everything in me, I wished I didn't have to do next, what I knew I had to do.

Gordon and I spent three hours in the apartment that first day—and that was plenty. Rather than immediately diving into the deep end of the pool, sorting and packing, we spent a portion of our time just trying to understand the scope of work.

The kitchen was quite small. There was no furniture or other items of critical significance in that space, other than some keys we found in a drawer. The refrigerator appeared to be working fine, so we decided not to disturb its contents.

In the main living area, a significant collection of books, artwork on the walls and other décor populated the space in contrast to a modest amount of furniture. The bedroom contained the bulk of the "mission-critical" items we would need to pack up—important documents and a significant amount of valuable personal items that shouldn't be left for would-be burglars.

When Gordon and I felt like we had reached our limit, we headed back across the Golden Gate Bridge and about a half hour north to the hotel I had booked. Dinner at a nearby restaurant afforded a much-needed change of scenery and time to decompress.

Over the next three days, we returned to Bill's apartment and continued sifting through stacks of paperwork and numerous bins and boxes. My brother had kept very detailed records of—everything; that was a blessing and a curse. Our paper chase was fruitful but tedious.

As we worked, my head was in the game and on task about half the time. The other half was spent trying to answer the many questions swirling around in my head like meat bees at a camp cookout.

On September 6, our third day at the condo, I received an unexpected text message from my contact at the mortuary, confirming he had taken possession of my brother's body. The message went on to state the internment was scheduled for that Friday, September 9.

The dispassionate wording in the message was somewhat jarring, but at the same time brought some much-needed comfort. It felt as though God had been watching Gordon and me working away in the condo. Aware I was lost in a fog, he extended a special touch of his grace through the closure of that matter.

That moment in time, six days after learning of my brother's death, was the first time I experienced any sense of peace. Later in the evening, I asked the Lord to continue to reveal himself at work in the midst of the madness as he had done for me in the past, and to draw me close.

The next day, Gordon and I drove out of the Pacific Heights neighborhood for the final time. We had packed the back of my truck full to the headliner with those banker's boxes full of paperwork and many personal items as well. As we left San Francisco, I was again so thankful to have my friend with me. Gordon's company and our conversations as we worked kept me sane.

I couldn't imagine spending five minutes alone in Bill's apartment.

Gordon had booked a 5:30 p.m. return flight to Southern California. We parted ways at the Sacramento airport about an hour before his flight, then I headed north for Cottonwood.

Over the past four days, my truck had been filled with moments of sorrow and frustration, but also good conversation and laughter. Yet as I began the trip north for home, I was struck by the nearly dead quiet enveloping me. Other than road noise, the only sound came from the heavy bankers boxes shifting and scuffing together in a soft chorus of white noise.

Not too far into the last leg of the drive home, I began feeling the physical and emotional impact of the trip. I was numb inside while my mind replayed a stream of images. I couldn't shake the one of the digital display on Bill's phone message machine silently flashing "30" in the dimly lit kitchen, like a voiceless scream in a nightmare.

Thirty messages left for my brother. One of them was mine. I had chosen not to play them back—just couldn't do it. But that decision left lingering questions.

Had Bill seen the flashing number and just walked away?

6

DIVING IN DEEP

Over the years I'd learned my best way to face daunting challenges was to pray for God's grace, his wisdom and his strength to face the fire, then dive in and do everything I could to own my situation so it didn't own me.

That had absolutely been the case when the blood cancer hit in 1989.

Other than getting hauled into the Principal's office at my elementary school for throwing a rock on the playground, it was the first time I had ever faced a life-threatening situation. The disease and treatment regimen tore through my six-month-old marriage like a tornado, leaving a wake of dreams tattered and tossed about, our finances in a tailspin and hope for a life on the other side of the storm foggy at best.

After completing six weeks as an inpatient at City of Hope National Medical Center in Duarte, California, I transitioned to their outpatient program. Each day, as I waited to report to the infusion clinic for my IV chemotherapy, I spent a couple of hours in the research library on the hospital campus. I perused as many articles, clinical research, medical textbooks, patient histories and any other relevant literature to learn all I could about Acute Lymphoblastic Leukemia.

When my cancer returned 19 and a half years later and I learned a bone marrow transplant was my only hope for survival, I employed the same tactic of diving in head first in order to understand and own as much of my circumstances as possible.

I was served with divorce papers two years after the cancer relapse, and again found myself in a situation where life took an unexpected hard left turn. My understanding of California divorce law was essentially non-existent. I knew I would need a competent attorney in my capacity as "Respondent," but also figured I had better bone up a bit on the relevant portions of the law for my own sanity.

Be it a medical condition, legal entanglement or some other life-altering issue, for my money there is no more frightening or frustrating position to be in than not understanding the full scope of the circumstances slapping you across the face. That was precisely how I felt within hours of learning of Bill's death.

For yet another time in my life, I figured I should dive in deep to avoid drowning.

Getting back home to Cottonwood at the end of the first four-day run to Bill's apartment was an important milestone—mentally, emotionally, psychologically and I suppose even spiritually. But when it came to the latter, I felt lost—a stunned believer standing in a smoking crater where his faith used to be.

Blink, blink.

My faith is central to who I am. Yet, from the moment I learned of my brother's death, the spiritual component—the prism through which I viewed myself, my life, others and the world— felt as if it had been jettisoned away like a spent rocket engine. I was out there in orbit, but felt zero connection with Mission Control.

Two days after returning home to Cottonwood, I received a

call from the clerk at the Cemetery office. She confirmed Bill's body had been interred and assured me every detail was executed according to my brother's expressed wishes.

I recall thanking the woman for her call, but doing so with my mind absolutely somewhere else. I'm not even sure I made much sense during our conversation. My brother's body was in the ground. That knowledge prompted a sense of relief, but also a profound sense of loss, perhaps for the first time since Bill's passing.

The thought I had lost my brother because he had taken his own life began to eat away at me.

I had no "theology of suicide."

Though I felt spiritually out of sorts, in the following days and weeks I dove in deep as much as possible in my role as executor of Bill's estate.

Certainly lacking passion, I prayed each day—for strength to hold up under the pressure, wisdom in my decision-making and peace as I wrestled with emotions and thoughts that seemed to soft boil my brain a little each day.

I sought and received a referral to an excellent attorney and booked an initial appointment at his San Francisco office to coincide with a second trip to Bill's apartment.

While addressing those matters, my mind repeatedly circled back to the 30 voice messages on Bill's answering machine. I hadn't stopped thinking about them since returning home. On more than one occasion, I told myself I should have sucked it up and listened to the messages. It might have made the task of putting together a notification list a bit easier—but I hadn't done that.

I spent time one day compiling a list of family members to notify about Bill's passing. Our cousins were scattered all over the country. I figured I had most of their current contact information, but I had very little information about my brother's friends. I searched for names Bill had mentioned in more recent history and searched as well for friends I recalled from his college years. I even tried to locate a few folks from his high school, Class of 1976.

How far back was too far, I wondered. *How far was far enough?*

I had found a few names on scraps of paper pinned to a bulletin board in Bill's apartment, but had no idea who those folks were. I thought perhaps I would find some answers during the second trip to his place.

7

CLEANING, SORTING AND FERAL CATS

Some good friends traveling throughout California were going to be heading back to Cottonwood on the same day I would be heading down to Bill's apartment for the next round of cleaning and packing. They offered to meet me in San Francisco and help with that effort.

I added a second room to my hotel reservation, and the three of us put in a couple of very full days at the apartment, sorting my brother's stuff into categories—Keep, Donate, Trash, etc. The second trip was when the deep cleaning began.

The refrigerator Gordon and I had decided not to mess with on our first foray into Bill's condo presented its own super fun challenges. We learned very quickly that disposing of spoiled, furry leftovers could drive one to consider cleaning solutions far beyond the realm of the reasonable—like a blowtorch, for example.

After a couple days of very productive work—including adding items to a detailed inventory initiated on the first trip to the condo—my friends and I concluded our efforts in the middle of a Wednesday afternoon. With their truck fully loaded with lots of Bill's stuff, my friends headed out on the last leg of their journey back to Cottonwood. I headed across town for the much-anticipated first meeting with the Probate attorney.

Driving away from my brother's place, I felt really good about what we accomplished and how much stuff we had been able to clear out of Bill's place. My truck was filled to the brim (again) with more boxes of paperwork and many items to be donated to charity.

Though I didn't know it at the time, very soon I would come to appreciate the heavy load I was hauling.

Three o'clock on a weekday afternoon wasn't the best time to join the crush of traffic making its way through the City. Thankfully, a short trip just three blocks south of Bill's place put me on Bush Street, heading east to my appointment relatively uncrushed.

The attorney's offices were on the 11th floor of a high rise tower located a block east of the famous Dragon Gate entrance to Chinatown. That part of the City can be a rolling frenzy of traffic and activity any time, any day. This day was no different.

As I approached the firm's Bush Street address, I joined a long line of vehicles in the right lane preparing to enter the parking garage adjacent to the tower. The cars participating in the impromptu "commerce parade" appeared to enter the garage at roughly five-second intervals. Ten cars from the entrance, all was right with the world. I would be right on time.

I drive a Toyota Sequoia, a fairly large SUV that can accommodate seven passengers when all the seats are in place. If the two back seats are removed, a large space becomes available for hauling a significant amount of cargo. Prior to the first trip to Bill's condo, I removed those seats so they could enjoy some quality time on Tony and Judy's front porch. After the second run to Bill's apartment, not only was the back end of the interior packed out, but the two middle row seats were folded forward like bad origami to accommodate the massive volume of stuff.

With just one car ahead of me in the parade, I glanced at the signage on the wall outside the garage entrance. Beyond the hours of operation sign, large block lettering alerted drivers of a seven-foot vertical clearance inside the parking structure.

I always paid close attention to that measurement as a metal cargo rack is mounted to the top of my truck. Unloaded and passenger-free, my vehicle stood six feet, eight inches tall, including the height of the rack. Heading into the garage I felt nothing but optimism about securing a parking space and making my way to the 11th floor of the tower. Again, all was right with the world.

Until...

The shriek of metal on metal scraping lasted just a couple seconds—long enough, I figured, for whatever I hit to drag across the entire length of the cargo rack.

So much for all being right with the world.

After peeling my face and palms from the inside of the windshield, I was struck with the realization I might be in real trouble.

The line of cars waiting behind me to enter the garage extended up Bush Street and passed two Starbucks Coffee shops —so, two full blocks. It wasn't like I had the option of backing out. Nope. I was a committed member of the "Church Of the Hunched Up and Praying" at that point and had to continue forward, scraping and all.

Inching along through the ground level, the struggling mathematician inside me wrestled with how a fully loaded SUV that empty, reached only six feet, eight inches in height could fail so miserably in a parking garage with a posted seven-foot clearance.

Was I one of the kids who was left behind in Math class?

Much to my relief, most of the plumbing and electrical infrastructure overhead was secured well above the cargo rack atop my vehicle. But every now and then, I was startled by more high-pitched shrieking that sounded less like metal-on-metal and more like my cargo rack had scraped the bottom of a bag of feral cats.

I spent nearly 15 minutes circling (and shrieking) up three levels of the parking structure before I found a space. Any sense of well-being was replaced by concerns I might be bounced from the law firm for missing the appointment window.

When I entered the tower's elevator, a rush of thankfulness washed over me. I was so thankful for the load my truck was hauling and the precious inch or so of reduced height it had afforded. I didn't want to even think about the three-story nightmare barely averted.

A seven-foot vertical clearance? Perhaps someone needed a new tape measure.

I entered the law firm's offices and was taken aback by the stunning view of San Francisco from the 11th floor of the tower. I'm pretty sure I was able to see all 97 Starbuck's coffee shop locations. I stated my name and was greeted warmly by the receptionist.

After just enough time to notice the richly appointed office décor, a well-dressed fellow introduced himself as "Matthew." He was the top dog—the man I had endured the screams of feral cats to meet.

Matthew led me to a small conference room. A woman soon joined us and introduced herself as Debra, one of the firm's attorneys and the person who would be my primary point of contact throughout the probate process.

I pulled a small notepad and pen from my backpack and settled in for what I expected to be a crash course in Probate Law. We met for about an hour that afternoon. Matthew and Debra walked me through the basics of probate. It was going to

Cleaning, Sorting and Feral Cats

be a long haul but Debra was quick to assure me there was no requirement that I be an expert in the law. I needed only to follow her directives in my capacity as executor of Bill's estate.

Within a few days of returning home, I would need to provide Debra with the original Last Will and Testament document my brother had sent me a year prior, along with one of the certified Death Certificates that arrived in the mail shortly after my initial conversation with the man at the mortuary.

Though the cause of death was left blank pending the results of the autopsy, the death certificate noted the date of Bill's passing. With those two documents in hand, Debra would file the Petition for Probate in the Superior Court.

A portion of the weight I had been carrying lifted. The probate process would be tedious but doable. The key to getting through it, I reckoned, was to take things one day at a time, keep my head down and follow orders.

First task up in the batting order—endure a second slow "crawl and scrape" through the parking garage of doom and head for home.

During my time in Bill's apartment on that second trip, I found an address book and several loose sheets of paper with a few familiar names and contact information. So, in the early days of October 2016, I placed calls to family members and friends to let them know of my brother's passing.

I chose not to share details about the note Bill left or the sleep aids and pain killers found on his nightstand—it just didn't feel right. Rather, I mentioned some serious medical issues he had been dealing with, which was not an untrue statement.

Those conversations overflowed with love and compassion. Countless times, folks commented about what a good person Bill was—what a gentle man he was. I was struck as well by how many of his friends mentioned how long they had known my brother and what a caring friend he had always been.

Hearing those comments and observations about Bill, in some cases from folks I had never met, blew me away. They painted a vivid picture of my brother I *needed* to see in my mind. A large block of my memories from the last decade of interactions with Bill were of conversations where frustrations mounted and issues remained unresolved, often with pieces of our differing viewpoints left broken and scattered on the floor.

In earlier years, our talks and interactions centered on many other aspects of life—good news and good things that were happening in our lives, personal and professional challenges and funny things that brought us both to our knees with laughter.

As I recalled *those* times, I found common ground with the folks who shared such heartfelt thoughts about my brother.

8

ON THE TREADMILL

Road trips to Bill's condo continued well into the final quarter of 2016. In spite of extensive sorting and dissemination of my brother's belongings—from clothing (lots of clothing) and household décor to pieces of furniture—a collection of his stuff began accumulating in and around Tony and Judy's home.

Many items had been donated to a charity that helped women in crisis rebuild their lives. Another batch of items were either donated to the Salvation Army or earmarked for disposal. And, of course, there were items I kept for sentimental reasons.

By the end of October, I had secured a storage locker near Cottonwood and was stunned by how quickly it filled up. Even after all that work, many boxes of stuff remained that ultimately required several years to sort through. As time and energy allowed, I spent time either at the storage locker or in my room at Tony and Judy's place, sometimes staring off into space but ultimately working through the contents of those boxes.

I often discovered items I wished I hadn't.

There were stacks of notes and letters, birthday and Christmas cards from family and friends, personal journals (I chose not to read) that spanned two decades, sketchpads, photo albums, corporate mementos and awards Bill received over the course of his career and more.

Over time, I realized those discoveries were a huge blessing from God. They helped paint a more complete picture of my brother and the life he had lived. In many instances, they brought back fond memories from our childhood or the many road trips and other great times we enjoyed in our adult years. I will always be grateful for that gift.

By mid-November of 2016, Operation "Clean Sweep" concluded. It had required five trips to Bill's condo and a trip to a storage locker he had rented near the San Francisco Airport to completely remove his footprint from the Bay Area.

It was about midway into the last quarter of the year when the probate work really took off. The bulk of my time each week was pretty much consumed by a seemingly constant in-flow of requests or instructions from Debra at the law firm. There were documents she needed, phone calls I had to make, letters to be written and myriad other tasks in my role as executor.

I was instructed to prepare a thorough inventory, declaring all of my brother's assets and their estimated "yard sale" value. Thankfully, that inventory had already been started on the first trip to Bill's place. Items believed to be of significant value had to be appraised and the appraiser's official paperwork included with my inventory.

I set up new checking and savings accounts to collect any remaining funds as Bill's various accounts were closed, then paid outstanding bills and expenses incurred in the consolidation of his estate.

There was a constant ebb and flow to the balances in those accounts, similar to how water was released from a reservoir in anticipation of spring snowmelt. On one occasion, I received a check for the remaining balance from a closed bank account, only to write a check the next day for nearly the same amount to pay off an outstanding credit card balance.

Many months of utility bill payments, hauling away and disposing of trash, (deep) cleaning and painting the condo, transport services to move Bill's car and some of his furniture to their new home in Cottonwood, a U-Haul truck rental and numerous incidental expenses had me cutting checks like a crazy man tossing dollar bills off the roof of a downtown high rise.

Everyone, please be patient. You'll get your money.

I wrote letters to every financial institution where Bill had active accounts to notify them of his passing, provide the required documentation, officially request the accounts be closed and provide information as to where any remaining funds should be sent. In some cases my letters were followed by multiple rounds of frustrating follow-up phone tag.

"Hi, guys. It's me, again."

"We're sorry, sir. We have no idea who you are until you can answer three security questions."

"Bro, again? We just hung up a few minutes ago."

The nagging questions surrounding my brother's death haunted me throughout the process. I had way more questions than answers and could not for the life of me understand—or shake off—the sense of spiritual disconnectedness I felt. There were moments on that treadmill where the pressure to perform got to be too much and I had to step off for a while—sometimes a long while.

Damn the Probate! All ahead full snore.

That work was by no means a well-oiled machine, but with God's grace I found a rhythm that allowed me to get a lot accomplished each week without my eyes rolling back too far in my head. I'm sure if my body had been wired directly into the electrical panel at Tony's house during that time, I could have provided more than enough juice to power his home—and perhaps his neighbor's place as well.

Who needs to install solar panels when there's a large man running on a hamster wheel 24/7 in the spare bedroom?

9

LOOKING BACK

The Decline

The last seven years of Bill's life coincided with the first seven following my bone marrow transplant in 2009. Those years were filled with numerous and consequential medical issues. My doctors referred to them as "known, expected complications and side effects."

I knew them only as "one thing after another."

My daily life often felt one-dimensional, as if reduced to a walk on a narrow path along a high mountain ridge with a sheer drop off on either side—eyes wide open and watch your step.

During that same period of time, my brother had been walking a similar path, fighting an ongoing and intensifying battle within himself.

On the night Bill was mugged, a doctor and social worker in the hospital's Emergency department strongly suggested I encourage my brother to connect with a brain injury recovery center across town. His head trauma was "significant," according to the doctor's assessment, and he believed Bill would benefit greatly from the clinic's specialized care.

I talked frequently with Bill in the weeks following the

mugging and began to notice the emotional toll that event had taken on him. There was a growing frustration inside him with life in San Francisco—really, life itself. He struggled to understand the callousness of his attacker and how easy it had been to become a victim of a crime.

Any encouragement from me or anyone else to pursue care at the clinic across town was met with opposition, from the timing not being right, concerns over insurance, finances and even genuine resignation—that it was simply "too late."

Unfortunately, that specialized care was never sought.

After our dad passed away in 1999, Bill took over the preparation of Mom's tax returns. For nearly two decades he had taken great pride in handling that aspect of our mom's care. But in 2014, he asked me to take on that responsibility, citing multiple reasons why he could no longer do the work.

And though he lived just 90 minutes away from our mom, he relied more and more on me to be her primary point of contact, be it a medical matter or simply visiting her and making sure she was doing okay.

Bill was slowly disengaging.

I was separated from Mom by several hundred miles, but tried to visit her as often as I could. Bill and I had to place her in a dementia care facility, as her physical and mental decline reached the point where she could no longer live in her own home.

After those visits, usually as I headed back home to Cottonwood, I always called Bill to give him a status update. For a while, those "After Action Mom Reports" were lots of fun. We laughed a bunch over funny things Mom had said or done.

Those conversations with my brother were perhaps our best and most enjoyable over the previous decade. Both of us were able to connect with and celebrate the *joy* of the moment.

But as Mom's health status continued to decline, I noticed a change in the tenor of my conversations with Bill. They became

Looking Back

less engaging, less enthusiastic and, more often than not, ended with both of us frustrated.

Granted, we were both feeling the pressure of caring for our mom while at the same time trying to manage our own lives, but there were occasions where I felt like I didn't know the person on the other end of the call.

I've wondered over the years if Bill ever thought the same of me.

In the early months of 2014, Mom's decline began to accelerate. Conversations and email exchanges with Bill about our mom became, at times, quite adversarial. A deep chasm opened between us. Our conversations became more "matter of fact," with much less personal interaction and hardly any joking.

As frustrated as I became with Bill, I'm sure he was equally frustrated with me—but not once did he ever express it. It almost would have been a relief if he had just once paused our conversation and let me have it: "Rob, enough. I don't think Mom's situation is as bad as you think it is."

In late June, Mom was approaching her 90th birthday. I put word out to some of her friends and coordinated with the staff at the care facility to arrange a little party. Part of the planning included a conversation with my brother to encourage him to attend the event.

Based on what I experienced during visits with Mom earlier in the year, I was convinced the Alzheimer's disease that had begun wrapping its tentacles around her over the previous four years was advancing at an alarming rate. In my gut, I felt she wouldn't be around too much longer.

Bill never gave me an answer, one way or the other, regarding attending Mom's party. Tony and Judy had history with Mom, so the three of us made the trip south together. My youngest daughter was planning on being there, so I looked forward to a great time celebrating Mom's special day. I could only hope Bill would decide the trip south from his place in the City was doable.

On the day of the party, Mom was in good spirits—stunned by the realization she had reached her 90th year, but absolutely loving all the fun. I brought down several birthday cards folks sent me to pass along to Mom. The facility staff baked a cake and joined us in singing "Happy Birthday." And though he arrived a bit late, Bill made the trip down and joined in the festivities.

I was so glad and so *relieved* to see him.

Reflecting on the event in the days that followed, I wrestled with some difficult realities.

Time spent with Mom that day confirmed her mental status was indeed declining at a faster pace. She still recognized me, my brother, her youngest granddaughter and Tony and Judy, but also asked several times why we were there and if we had come to take her home.

I felt a profound sense of loss, even though Mom was still very much alive.

Prior to Mom's party, I hadn't seen Bill in-person for several years. We had only talked on the phone or exchanged emails. He had made trips down from San Francisco to visit Mom on many occasions when she still lived in her own home and, for a while, after we made the difficult decision to place her in the care facility. But it was a rare occasion when Bill and I were together when we visited our mom.

Through my phone conversations and email exchanges with Bill, I had developed a mental picture of him and his life in San Francisco. During our interactions at the party, much of that mental snapshot was confirmed.

We still enjoyed some laughs and fun, but it felt as though Bill was having a most difficult time just "being," like he felt the crush of a million thoughts and concerns pressing in on him. He displayed a flat affect and appeared distracted, drawn and tired.

Mixed with the joy and happiness I felt that day, I was also

Looking Back

sad and felt a sense of helplessness. I didn't realize it at the time, but Mom's 90th birthday party was the beginning of "goodbye." It would be the final gathering of our family and the last time I would see my brother alive.

Over the next year, conversations with Bill became increasingly more difficult and frustrating. I knew he was in a world of hurt and growing more and more disillusioned with life. Sometimes I was able to sit quietly and listen as he shared what was on his mind. Other times, I found it nearly impossible to contain my frustration.

Was I being selfish? Was Bill being selfish?

I and several other folks who knew Bill and had history with him had offered suggestions for how he might be able to find some relief from the pressure-cooker he repeatedly described as his life. On one occasion, Bill was really down about living in San Francisco. He told me he was fast approaching his limit of cold and fog, the isolation and detachment he felt, and his inability to keep his life from spiraling out of control.

He knew he was in real trouble.

Bill commented it had been several years since he enjoyed quality sleep in his condo. I asked if he had ever considered renting a suite for a month or so at a hotel outside the City. Initially, Bill responded positively to the idea. He seemed to like the notion of putting some physical (and mental, emotional and psychological) distance between himself and the only world he had known since 1997.

But just as quickly as he had amped up over the idea, he shot it down, citing multiple reasons why it wasn't a good idea. That kind of resistance became Bill's default response to any attempts to help him.

As his downward spiral continued, the only ideas Bill would consider when we talked were his own. Part of me understood that my efforts and those of family members and friends to offer support and encouragement were most likely doomed, long before the last digit in his phone number had even been entered. And I was okay with that—kind of.

But another part of me grew more and more exasperated. I was trying to support my brother, while trying to figure out what life on the other side of the divorce was supposed to look like and, at the same time, address new and recurring medical problems related to the bone marrow transplant.

Those medical problems pretty much owned me throughout 2015 and into 2016. I was forced to confront post-transplant side-effects that initially reared their ugly head in 2013. Back then, a bagel-shaped growth about the size of a nickel grew out of the top of my head—out of thin air.

What?

At the appointment to remove the demon mini-bagel, I learned an anti-fungal medication I was prescribed following my transplant four years earlier had a dark side that was just coming to light in the medical community. For immune-compromised patients, the med could cause Basil and Squamous Cell Carcinomas, Pleomorphic Sarcomas (those are fun) and a host of other nasty little things best left out of the dinner table conversation, to spring forth from a patient's head… and ears… and face… and neck… and (bonus) internally as well.

Playing skin tumor dodgeball and enduring long-term, "scorched earth" topical treatments and archeological digs to remove cancerous growths, took a physical and emotional toll. It sucked a lot of energy from me and made it difficult to keep all the balls I was juggling in the air.

It also became increasingly more difficult to spend long periods of time on the phone with my brother, regardless of who initiated the call. He was only interested in reviewing his growing list of grievances about the city in which he lived, his home, the (terrible) weather, regrets over bad decisions he felt he made decades earlier and more.

The list of worries grew each time we talked. Though my heart broke for him, a time came when I had to establish a time limit boundary of 15 minutes for our conversations. Beyond that, they typically descended into a really bad place for both of us.

The Tailspin

In late 2015, I received a call from Brian, one of Bill's long-time friends who was concerned about the changes in his friend of more than 30 years. We talked for a long time. Brian was deeply concerned that Bill's status was in rapid decline, that he was withdrawing into himself and deteriorating at an alarming pace.

Brian apologized for reaching out to me. I assured him I welcomed his call and was so glad he felt comfortable doing so. What prompted his call that particular day was a dramatic change he noticed in my brother's behavior. Brian traveled frequently, and when he knew he would be in San Francisco for a spell, would always contact Bill to meet for dinner; this had long been their routine.

But on the day Brian contacted me, he had recently spoken with Bill where, for the first time in the history of their friendship, Bill declined his friend's invitation. Bill told him it wasn't a good time for them to get together, and during the conversation didn't sound or seem like the friend Brian had known for so long.

We shared observations about our respective recent interactions with Bill, along with thoughts about what next steps might be necessary. Before we ended our conversation, I assured Brian I would keep him posted on any new developments. He promised to do the same.

Brian and I shared a mutual frustration over not knowing exactly what to do. We were a brother and a good friend separated by hundreds of miles, wanting only to help a guy we both cared about immensely, but feeling rather powerless to do so.

After ending the conversation, I realized a "countdown clock" of sorts had been quietly ticking away in the background of my brother's life. That ticking seemed to be getting louder with each passing day. Time to help Bill was dwindling.

By the end of spring in 2016, thoughts about my brother's situation yielded fewer and fewer ideas about how to help him. My "tank" was about empty. *How much more empty*, I wondered, *was my brother's?*

The frequency of our interactions via phone and email had declined dramatically since the beginning of the year. I prayed for a miracle—for the Lord to heal Bill and stop the tailspin his life had descended into. And I asked God to help me do what I could to help my brother.

On June 24th, I received a new text message from Bill's friend, Brian. Since our conversation in 2015, he had experienced the same distancing and lack of communication with Bill as I had. He hadn't heard from Bill in weeks. "Not a good sign," Brian wrote. I shared that other than having received some Trust-related documentation from Bill in recent history, I had not had direct communication with him since mid-May.

About a week prior to my text exchange with Brian, I had met up with my youngest daughter in the Bay Area to visit Mom. I took a photo of the two of them and emailed it to Bill. But my message had bounced back as undeliverable, pending verification of my identity and proof I was a real person. That was something new.

Brian and I were in total agreement about my brother's declining status. He concluded our text conversation with a sobering thought: "Intervention might be the only next step."

The next day, in a moment of near desperation, I reached out to a cousin on my dad's side of the family tree. Earl—Dr. Earl—was a licensed marriage and family therapist with a doctorate in clinical psychology. He headed a Christian counseling group in Southern California. He'd written seven books, co-authored three more and had a million+ followers through social media.

For the past two decades, Dr. Earl had been working closely with brain imaging research pioneer Daniel G. Amen, MD. The Amen Clinics were integrating unique brain imaging technology into the treatment of psychological, physical and even spiritual problems. They had helped countless individuals suffering from a wide range of issues, among them, traumatic brain injury (TBI).

To this day, I'm at a loss to explain why the thought of contacting Earl hadn't crossed my mind any sooner than it did.

I first met Earl in the early 1980s, when he moved to California from Minnesota to pursue his doctorate. Soon after arriving he looked up my dad, eager to connect with a relative and fellow Minnesotan. He and Dad became fast friends and enjoyed many years of connection before Dad passed away in 1999.

Earl and I had been in contact with each other on many occasions in the years that followed. Yet, even with that history and family connection, I felt a bit awkward about contacting him regarding my brother. I didn't want to impose.

I texted Earl and asked if it might be possible for the two of us to talk. Earl's response was immediate and gracious.

"Happy to help you, Rob. Give me a call."

That conversation opened a door to new possibilities for getting Bill some real help. When I told Earl that Bill had suffered a concussion when he was mugged in 2010, Earl was confident Bill could benefit from the work he and Dr. Amen were doing.

I thought perhaps all was not lost, that my brother might finally get the help he so desperately needed—in spite of that ticking clock.

Earl and I worked together long-distance to construct as much of a patient profile of Bill as was possible. Earl's goal was to get him down to Southern California to receive the specialized brain care at the Amen Clinics.

It was during that time I began to learn the harsh realities of traumatic brain injuries and their potentially life-altering impact.

During one of my conversations with Earl, he shared that the human brain has the consistency of mashed potatoes, and the sudden jarring of the brain from a concussion actually changes the brain's chemistry.

Even a mild concussion—a single event—had the potential to ruin a person's life.

I dug deeper into the nature of concussions. Inside the seeming fortress of the skull, the brain—that fragile batch of mashed potatoes—is essentially suspended in cerebrospinal fluid. When the brain is traumatized by a concussion "either a direct impact or whiplash effect causes the brain to move inside the head and bump against the skull.

As a result, neurons are damaged and the brain may bruise at the site of impact. The required force is surprisingly minimal...."[1]

I watched the 2015 film, *Concussion*, a real-life account of the ground-breaking work of neuropathologist Dr. Bennet Omalu into the brain damage inflicted on professional football players from repetitive concussions over the course of their careers.

The movie brought national awareness to the issue. It most definitely captured my attention, as I saw similarities in some of the thought patterns and behaviors of well-known football players portrayed in the film and what I was experiencing with my brother.

Traumatic brain injuries could trigger psychiatric disorders such as "anxiety, depression, substance abuse, and panic disorder along with homelessness, domestic violence, divorce, and suicide. Furthermore, untreated brain injuries [could] lead to Alzheimer's disease and other dementias."[2]

Looking Back

In some cases, a concussion could have a long-term impact. The long-term complications of concussion include:

- Post-concussion syndrome. This is a condition in which [one experiences] concussion symptoms for weeks or even months (instead of days) after experiencing a concussion. Such symptoms may include ongoing dizziness/spinning, headache, memory and concentration problems, mood swings, depression, anxiety, irritability, personality changes, insomnia (can't sleep) and excessive drowsiness.
- Higher risk of anxiety and depression (especially if there's been multiple concussions).
- Structural brain injuries from multiple concussions. People who have had several head injuries in their life are at higher risk of long-lasting impairment. Chronic traumatic encephalopathy is one example of a brain condition linked to repeated blows to the head.
- Problems with memory, naming and word-finding.
- Dementia."[3]

As I learned about the damaging effects of concussions, Bill's resistance to seeking follow-up care from the brain clinic in San Francisco echoed hauntingly in the back of my mind.

As Earl worked behind the scenes in Southern California, Bill's personal crises and critical matters related to the fiduciary responsibilities we shared as co-trustees of our family Trust strained our relationship nearly to the breaking point. I did my best to support my brother and bridge the chasm that had developed between us, but it was tough sledding.

We were both running on vapors.

In what would be one of the last phone conversations I

would have with my brother, I told Bill I had reached out to our cousin Earl to get his input and perhaps some real help. Bill acknowledged he knew he was in real trouble and had been struggling to even carry out the simplest of tasks.

At first, he responded positively to the idea of working with Earl, but rather quickly dismissed the notion with resigned comments about "what might have been possible" if he had talked with Earl years ago. In Bill's mind, the time to get help had long passed. I tried to encourage him, but it felt like my words fell on deaf ears.

Bill and I exchanged only a few emails over the remainder of the summer of 2016. In many instances, several days or even weeks preceded any response. If I called to follow up, more often than not I was forced to "leave a message after the beep." The last time I did that was August 24th—Bill's 58th birthday.

I never heard from him again.

10

WANDERINGS

Fear not, for I am with you;
Be not dismayed, for I am your God.
I will strengthen you,
Yes, I will help you,
I will uphold you with My righteous right hand.

— ISAIAH 41:10

On December 12, 2016, just three and a half months after Bill's death, Mom passed away. God had blessed her with 92 full years of life as a loving wife, mother and grandmother. And just days before her passing, Mom learned she was also a great grandmother as she held my youngest daughter's newborn baby girl in her arms.

Mom passed peacefully in her sleep. She had a rock solid faith and had been a true prayer warrior. I was crushed by her passing but knew she was welcomed into God's loving presence as a good and faithful servant. I could only imagine the joy she experienced when she was reunited with Dad, my brother and so many other family members and friends.

Christmas that year was a time of sadness more than joy. I

missed my brother, my mom—my whole family, really. On Christmas Day I was surrounded by the warmth and love of an amazing group of friends, but in the quiet moments it was difficult to grasp the reality I was the only remaining member of my immediate family.

That day was the first day I thought about how best to honor the lives of my brother and my mom.

Given the responsibilities already on my plate, and with friends and relatives scattered across the country, planning a memorial service—perhaps two of them—was more than my personal power grid could handle. I had to trust the matter would work itself out as it was meant to.

At the start of the New Year, I began work to close out the family Trust. My time each day was split between those new responsibilities and slogging through the remaining items to be addressed as executor of Bill's estate. I felt numb to my core, just going through the motions each day. I made it to church on Sunday mornings about 20 percent of the time. And when I was there, more often than not my heart and mind were someplace else.

When I faced the challenges I had encountered over the years, God's words in the Old Testament book of Isaiah (41:10) had become one of my go-to, solid rock reminders that he had me in his grip—even in the midst of the most confounding circumstances.

When Mom passed, I found peace and comfort in the promises of Isaiah 41:10. But whenever I thought about the death of my only brother to suicide, the meaning and promises in that verse and others like it seemed to lose all resonance, like I was reading empty words—ink on paper.

I feared. I was dismayed.

I prayed each day the Lord would grant me strength to do the work I was charged to do—for both estates. I prayed he would provide answers to my questions, but I was unsettled, untethered.

Were those hollow, faithless prayers? I didn't know.

I found some relief from the grind through work on a new book project I had undertaken a couple years prior—a photo collection and travel log of sorts. It was an energizing and creative pursuit and a departure from the other books I had written.

The joy I found through that endeavor was a perfect counter to the weight of daily life and the often disconnectedness of my spiritual wanderings. Through that project I found a fitting way to honor the lives of my brother and my mom. It was an answer to prayer.

Bill and Mom had both been blessed with many creative talents, among them, wonderful drawing and painting skills. They produced beautiful works over the course of their lives. When I published the new book, *Natural Selections* in September of 2017, tributes to both of them, along with samples of some of their work, were included in the back matter.

Following are those two tributes.

Bill Henslin
1958 – 2016

I was always amazed by my brother Bill's artistic ability. He was meticulous about the details, be it a pencil rendering of a mountain scene, or a seascape rendered in oils or acrylics.

I was the one who cracked open a sketchpad and hurriedly whipped out a drawing. My brother was the guy who spent hours, creek side in a lawn chair, rendering every detail of the rocks visible just below the surface of the water.

A bank in the city where we were raised hosted an annual art show and contest. Students from the high school submitted entries across a variety of categories. During my four years, I submitted several pieces, and received some really dandy "Honorable Mention" ribbons. Those were essentially "participation trophies" awarded to kids who showed up, gave it all they had but in the end, were smoked like a cheap cigar by someone who really had the chops.

But a few years before my participation in the art show, my brother made his run at it. In 1976, his senior year, Bill received a First Place ribbon for a large, acrylic painting of the Santa Barbara harbor. His art teacher was so blown away by it she wanted to buy the piece to display in her home.

But that was just the start. That same year, Bill's seascape oil painting took home the Best of Show honors. His painting hung on the main wall of the bank, in all its glory, for a full year. Whenever I went into the place, I was full of pride over what my big brother had accomplished.

In the years after high school and college, Bill continued his creative pursuits. He had a vision for renovating old homes to their former glory and used his own home in Washington State as a proving ground for that notion. With the same meticulous attention to detail he had when he was a kid, my brother turned an old '50s bungalow into a stunner of a home.

Bill excelled in drawing, painting, remodeling, interior design and photography as well. He was an authentic creative and a great guy. Though he is gone, his memory will remain alive through the beautiful art he left behind.

Jeanne Henslin
1924 - 2016

Painter Agnes Martin once said, "My paintings are not about what is seen. They are about what is known forever in the mind."

For my mom, Jeanne, what was known in her mind, what she loved and appreciated, was reflected in her creative pursuits. She was a talented creative, and when she was not engaged in the regular activities of life, marriage and raising her two sons, she pursued drawing, painting, writing and music with great joy and enthusiasm.

Dreams of becoming a fashion illustrator occupied her mind as a young girl. In her early twenties, she paid for studio time at CBS Records, boarded a bus to downtown Los Angeles and recorded an album of American classics.

Throughout her adult years, Jeanne fanned the flames of her creative passions whenever possible. She wrote short stories, and was so excited to learn one day that a story had been accepted for publication.

When my brother and I were in college, Mom decided to write her life's story and bound printed copies for us. Years later, my young daughters often asked if their bedtime story could be portions of their Grandma Jeanne's memoirs.

Some of Mom's most fond memories were of childhood summers spent camping at Carpinteria State Beach on the central California coast. Those memories were "known forever in [her] mind" as she developed her skills in watercolor painting.

Her subject matter was usually ocean and beach scenes —crashing waves on storm-battered rock outcroppings, seagulls in flight against sunset skies, still life studies of a single starfish or other seashell or the delicate rendering of wet sand and shells left behind as the remnant of a broken wave receded back into the ocean.

Mom was a very private person, and as much as that dynamic existed in her creative pursuits, she was also a very caring and giving person. She enjoyed sharing her artistic discoveries and endeavors with friends and family, often revealing works in progress or framing paintings as gifts.

Throughout her life, in all she did, Mom was driven by what was "known forever in [her] mind," that life was a tremendous blessing, that the "stuff" of life—family, friends, the beauty of creation expressed in the intricate design of a seashell or the lapping of tidewaters on a stretch of beach, should be celebrated and shared.

11

TRYING TO MAKE SENSE OF IT ALL

One of the most frustrating things I've wrestled with since my brother's passing, is the reality I had been well aware of his decline. I engaged with him for years in an effort to help him find a light in the darkness that seemed to be engulfing him, knowing full well there was only so much I could do beyond offering brotherly encouragement and support.

The possibility of some kind of intervention to help Bill in the final months of his life faded away as his opposition to any offerings of help grew more and more dismissive.

As I sought answers in the wake of Bill's death, I was impacted by the following suicide statistics:

> "Every day, approximately 123 people in the U.S. die by suicide, making it the 10th leading cause of death. Among people aged 10-34, suicide is the second leading cause of death. And it ranks as the fourth leading cause of death in those between 35 and 54 years of age. In 2017, twice as many Americans died by suicide than by homicide."[1]

I read that paragraph once, in an online article, then just stared at it in disbelief.

123 people each day—nearly 45,000 people every year—chose to end their own lives. Awkwardly, I wondered about the other 122 folks who took their lives on the day my brother took his. *What struggles had they endured? What demons had tormented them? How long had they fought before deciding they were done?*

The American Foundation for Suicide Prevention (AFSP), identified a number of health, environmental and historical **risk factors** that increase the chances that an individual may attempt suicide. Here is that list:

Health

- Mental health conditions
- Depression
- Substance use problems
- Bipolar disorder
- Schizophrenia
- Personality traits of aggression, mood changes and poor relationships
- Conduct disorder
- Anxiety disorders
- Serious physical health conditions including pain
- Traumatic brain injury

Environmental

- Access to lethal means including firearms and drugs
- Prolonged stress, such as harassment, bullying, relationship problems or unemployment
- Stressful life events, like rejection, divorce, financial crisis, other life transitions or loss
- Exposure to another person's suicide, or to graphic or sensationalized accounts of suicide

Historical

- Previous suicide attempts
- Family history of suicide
- Childhood abuse, neglect or trauma

Protective Factors

- Access to mental health care, and being proactive about mental health
- Feeling connected to family and community support
- Problem-solving and coping skills
- Limited access to lethal means
- Cultural and religious beliefs that encourage connecting and help-seeking, discourage suicidal behavior, or create a strong sense of purpose or self-esteem.[2]

On one level I was frustrated by the AFSP's materials, as I didn't have a crystal ball or other means of understanding the totality of my brother's life. I wanted so much to fill in all the blanks but that wasn't possible. But on another level, I was thankful to have found good information that helped me begin to make sense of Bill's death.

Bill tended to be more of a private person—not one to lay all his cards on the table—especially when it came to his personal life. That said, there had been many conversations over the decades where we both shared from the heart about the challenges we were facing.

The memory of some of those conversations, as well as my more recent interactions with Bill in the last years of his life (especially those following the concussion), helped me get past those "crystal ball" frustrations and identify several risk factors that were part of the fabric of my brother's life. It was a hard bit of reality to swallow.

I won't detail the specifics of what I identified. I can only state that in my heart I'm convinced my brother had been living for years—perhaps decades—under the weight of significant personal challenges that absolutely played a role in his decision to end his life.

The concussion Bill suffered when he was mugged only exacerbated his situation. If I spend too much time thinking about that aspect of his decline, the broken, fallen part of me still chomps at the bit for five minutes of quality time with the guy who jumped him.

Lord, please forgive me.

In addition to suicide risk factors, the AFSP identified a number of potential **warning signs** that someone might be contemplating suicide:

Warning signs

Something to look out for when concerned that a person may be suicidal is a change in behavior or the presence of entirely new behaviors. This is of sharpest concern if the new or changed behavior is related to a painful event, loss, or change. Most people who take their lives exhibit one or more warning signs, either through what they say or what they do.

Talk

If a person talks about:

- Killing themselves
- Feeling hopeless
- Having no reason to live
- Being a burden to others

- Feeling trapped
- Unbearable pain

Behavior

Behaviors that may signal risk, especially if related to a painful event, loss or change:

- Increased use of alcohol or drugs
- Looking for a way to end their lives, such as searching online for methods
- Withdrawing from activities
- Isolating from family and friends
- Sleeping too much or too little
- Visiting or calling people to say goodbye
- Giving away prized possessions
- Aggression
- Fatigue

Mood

People who are considering suicide often display one or more of the following moods:

- Depression
- Anxiety
- Loss of interest
- Irritability
- Humiliation/Shame
- Agitation/Anger
- Relief/Sudden Improvement[3]

Viewed through the filter of the AFSP's warning signs, memories of interactions I had with my brother over the last decade of his life fostered a sense of dread inside me. The warning signs had been there—some in plain sight—but I hadn't recognized them for what they were.

As difficult as they were to swallow, the AFSP's lists of suicide risk factors and warning signs helped me better understand and contextualize the changes I experienced in Bill's talk, behavior and mood as his status declined.

On the cusp of the five-year anniversary of Bill's passing, I had a phone conversation with a good friend about all that had transpired since losing Bill and Mom. Over the course of our 30-year friendship, my friend and I had engaged in many conversations about life and matters of faith, especially as it related to our mutual journeys with persistent medical challenges and chronic illness.

Among several topics discussed that day, we talked about grieving loss and other difficulties that befall us and how grieving was a *process*. I shared that even at the fifth anniversary of Bill's death, I was still a mess and hadn't been able to put all the broken pieces back together.

At one point in our conversation my friend commented, "I don't think we Christians in the present age do well at all with *lament*."

She had my full attention as she continued.

"Lament played such an important role in the lives of the ancient Israelites. A large portion of the songs in the book of Psalms are songs of lament. But how much time do we give lament in our church services, our prayer life or in Bible study?"

After our conversation, I reflected on my friend's comment, the challenges I had faced over the years, and how I had been able to identify my progression through the classic Kübler-Ross model of the Five Stages of Grief: Denial, Anger, Bargaining, Depression and Acceptance.

Was that progression a journey of lament?

Swiss-American psychiatrist Elisabeth Kübler-Ross developed the model through her work with the terminally ill, where she observed a commonality of five distinct responses among her patients. She presented the model for the first time in her book, *On Death and Dying* published in 1969.

Though originally developed to assist those facing eminent death, the model had been used to help individuals process a variety of traumatic events such as crime victimization, disease and disability, divorce, financial difficulties, job change and more.

An article from the North Carolina-based Jonas Hill Hospital and Clinics provided an excellent summary of the five stages of grief as they relate to the loss of a loved one.

1. Denial and Isolation

The first stage of grief is denial. This is usually accompanied by isolation. During this stage, it is normal for people to think that there is no way the situation can be real. This is usually a reflexive response to hearing about the loss of a loved one. People instantly respond with denial, thinking that there is no way the person is gone.

As other people continue to tell this person that their loved one has passed away, they run away from these people to avoid these statements. This is where the isolation comes from. Eventually, people progress out of this first stage and move to the second one.

2. Anger

The second stage of grief is anger. This anger does not necessarily have to be at the death of the loved one. Nearly anyone, or anything, can be the target of this anger. This anger could be aimed at inanimate objects. It might be aimed at total strangers. Individuals often get angry at family members and friends.

Importantly, this anger is not a way to place blame, but is simply a coping mechanism. Individuals do not want to accept the reality of the situation and get angry with the world in general. Eventually, people vent this anger and move to the third stage of grief.

3. Bargaining

The third stage of grief is bargaining. People who are going through grief will bargain with just about anyone or anything. Even though people going through grief often bargain in a religious setting, hoping to rectify the situation, they will also bargain with family members and friends, knowing that they have no control over the situation.

This is often where feelings of guilt start to show up. Statements usually start with "if only," such as "if only we had stopped him from getting in that car," or "if only we had sought medical care sooner." These are common signs that someone is going through the bargaining stage of grief. Eventually, this bargaining will cease and the next stage will appear.

4. Depression

Depression is the fourth stage of grief. It is a common and serious medical issue. Some of the most common signs of depression include:

- Changes in sleep, either sleeping more or sleeping less
- Changes in eating habits, either eating more or eating less
- Massive feelings of guilt, regardless of whether they are justified
- A loss of enjoyment in activities that used to bring pleasure
- Thoughts of suicide...

5. Acceptance

The last stage of grief is called acceptance. This phase is marked by withdrawal and calm. This is not a period of happiness but it must be distinguished from depression. Acceptance does not have the symptoms of depression listed above.

This does not mean that the individual is at peace with the loss of a loved one, but does mark a movement away from depression.[4]

It's important to note that individual experiences with each stage in that framework may be linear in nature as described above, or they may not. As each of us is unique, so is the manner in which we encounter and process difficult, life-altering circumstances.

My three-decade-long journey through those stages had been less linear in nature, more closely resembling a recombinant dance of sorts. Whether trying to cope with devastating medical issues, the pain of my divorce—and even in good times, when I believed my head and heart were in a good place—manifestations of the stages of grief would surface then subside, like whales breeching otherwise calm seas.

Hello! Remember us?

I was both intrigued and confused by my friend's comments about lament. I thought I had engaged in some type of grieving over the past 30 years—the Kübler-Ross model was all too familiar. And I prayed many prayers during the difficult times, and saw God's miracles and his blessings. He was faithful. He strengthened and upheld me, just as Isaiah 41:10 promised. Waking up each day and realizing I was still alive and the father of two miracle daughters was pretty much a daily reminder of that reality.

Utilizing the Kübler-Ross grief model to process my pain was similar, I thought, to what my friend had stated about lament. But five years after my brother's death, I was still a spiritual train wreck. There were many occasions where, in spite of "grieving," I felt tremendous (perhaps self-inflicted) pressure to shrug off my pain and just get on with life.

I was floundering.

After my friend shared her insights about lament, my brain sizzled with promptings to take time—*make* time—to learn about it. I was able to dismiss them for a while, as life at the time already had my full attention. But eventually the need to make sense of my spiritual "funk" won the battle of wills.

12

LAMENT

When I began my study of lament, two realities soon occupied space in my mind. First, though I had earned an undergraduate degree in Religious Studies (a lifetime ago), I was *not* a biblical scholar—not even close. Second, I was no longer in my early twenties and able to burn the candle at both ends.

The success of this endeavor would require three things: humility, fiber and naps.

I established a contemporary, baseline definition of "lament." Several popular dictionaries define the word as both a noun and verb. As a noun, a lament is a dirge, hymn, prayer, poem or song. In its verb forms, to lament is to express grief or sorrow, mourn, regret deeply or wail. I never encountered definitions or characterizations of lament as "whining" or "complaining;" Lament, it seemed came from a deeper place.

The majority of lament content in the Bible is found primarily within the pages of two books in the old testament—Lamentations and Psalms.

The book of Lamentations is just five chapters in length with a narrative devoted entirely to the subject of lament. In contrast, the book of Psalms—the longest book in the Bible—contains 150 psalms (or hymns) that address a wide range of issues—some joyful and celebratory, others mournful and reflective. About forty percent of the psalms are psalms of lament that cry out to God about some of life's most heart-wrenching issues: accusations, illness, oppression, sin and repentance.

While engaged in my studies, I often thought about the phone conversation with my friend—how she emphasized the importance of lament in the old testament. The *practice* of lament —praying, singing and speaking those prayers from the depths of an anguished soul—was an essential step in the healing process, regardless of the source of anguish. Lament was and is today the fullest, deepest and perhaps most genuine expression of grief.

Though I had studied the book of Psalms and the book of Lamentations in college, the significance of lament in the lives of the ancient Israelites hadn't impacted me personally. But reading them with the loss of my only brother still fresh in my mind and heart, the impact was profound.

I had prayed a thousand prayers over the course of my life—many from a place of joy and thanksgiving—but plenty from a place of pain. My prayers during the dark times were prayers for strength and endurance. But there had never been an occasion where, in the midst of those difficulties, I was *deliberate in grieving* the heartache and hardships—the sense of loss.

Initially, I was frustrated by that realization. But ultimately, my study of lament revealed three truths that fostered a profound respect for the practice that I know will help me in the days to come.

First, **lament affords an opportunity to take healthy, appropriate *action*** in the midst of dire circumstances. I had relied on the Kübler-Ross model of the five stages of grief to get a sense—a snapshot—of my attitudes, feelings and thoughts. But awareness (information) is passive in nature. In contrast, *lament* is a living, breathing tool we can use to turn *awareness* into *action* by articulating our grief.

Second, **lament is an ordered and intentional process.** The verses in the 60 psalms of lament utilize a well-organized structure, based on the sequence of letters in the Hebrew alphabet. And in Lamentations, grief is fully expressed over five separate laments, each written from a different point of view expressed through ordered and intentional structures. This allows for the full expression of grief.

Third, **lament makes room for *hope*.** The psalmists initially engage God at the height of their despair. And though their soul-crushing circumstances may have continued for a time, the overwhelming majority of their laments conclude in confident hope of resolution and restoration by God.

A note to readers—I've included a more detailed study of lament in the Appendix of this book.

13

REALIZATIONS

I referenced an extensive bibliography of articles, Bible commentaries, books and sermons in my study of lament. One article in particular seemed to crystalize the importance of the practice. Entitled, *Lament: A Path to Healing*, professional counselor Karen Weeks writes,

> "Good mental and emotional health involves grieving our losses and disappointments. I'm not an advocate of 'wallowing' in despair, or throwing a never-ending pity party for ourselves, but I also don't believe we can just "move forward" without truly getting honest about our feelings. When we don't allow ourselves to grieve, we often have to harden our hearts in order to move on and pretend everything is fine. But that does nothing to help us have an authentic relationship with God, ourselves, or others. Unless we allow ourselves time and space to lament, our wounds and disappointments will turn to bitterness and resentment."[1]

After reading the article, I considered the author's reference to "moving forward." It seemed that mindset had permeated contemporary society. At its core were two foundational premises: dismiss pain and suck it up.

Grieving brought pain. Pain was bad. Instead, we directed our energies on the things we had to do, the places we had to go and anything else we could find to occupy our frazzled minds and broken spirits. We focused on keeping pace with the unceasing pulse of life.

With fists clenched, we stood before our microwave ovens, incensed over the two minutes required to pop a bag of popcorn—we hadn't the time nor patience for such nonsense. We were way too busy "getting over" hardships, stuffing pain down deeper and deeper inside ourselves so we could keep "moving forward."

To help us on our frenzied journeys, bookstores offered a seemingly endless smorgasbord of advice and counsel to help us achieve "balance" and peace in our lives, find meaning and discern our true purpose—the whole ball of wax—and in just seven easy steps. I had some of those books on my bookshelf; one of them included a diagram of the Five Stages of Grief.

Sheesh!

Over the course of my life, I had prayed many prayers for myself and others. In good times and in bad, I believed the promises of God, like those in Isaiah 41:10 and so many others.

I tried to live each day I was granted to the fullest, be it a good day or bad.

When my wife and I received the grim news that leukemia had invaded my body, we prayed for grace and strength to endure the utter turmoil the illness brought to our young marriage.

During the most difficult days of treatment, when I didn't care if I survived or not, I prayed and thanked God for his promises to be with me and sustain me. I thanked him for the thousands of folks across the country who prayed for my full recovery.

I tried to "move forward" and live each day I was granted to the fullest, be it a good day or bad.

I offered up prayers of thanksgiving and praise when my first battle with blood cancer concluded and I returned to work. When God blessed my wife and I with two miracle daughters, I was overwhelmed with joy.

When the cancer returned after nearly two decades in remission, I prayed for wisdom and strength to endure the treatment. On the other side of that nightmare, I thanked God for bringing me through the bone marrow transplant and adding days and years to my life.

When my marriage fell apart, I prayed for guidance to find my way through that fog. I had tried to look past the pain and focus on the hope of better days to come.

When transplant-related complications repeatedly put me back in the hospital and when my mom's health began to decline, I prayed for God's grace and strength.

I tried to "move forward" and "dive in deep," and live each day I was granted to the fullest, be it a good day or bad.

The Five Stages of Grief was the framework I used to process the roller coaster that was my life. I prayed for clarity and purpose to find the greener pastures of a "new normal" I hoped lay just beyond the horizon. And when I prayed, I believed my prayers were heard. I believed God had not lost his grip on me and still held me in his loving arms. The promises of Isaiah 41:10 were legit.

I knew it in the depths of my soul.

Then one day I complained about how long it took to microwave a packet of popcorn. I hadn't the time nor patience for such delays—I was "moving forward" to live each day I was granted to the fullest, be it a good day or bad.

That's what I was supposed to do, right?

Then one day my brother took his own life, and my faith crashed and burned.

I felt numb, disconnected and hollow. When I prayed, more often than not my words felt almost meaningless—I hadn't a clue why. Without realizing it, I bought into that flawed "move forward" mentality. I didn't want to endure another season of pain—not again.

This one hurt too much.

My spiritual disintegration had everything to do with a weapons-grade desire to shrug off my brother's suicide as another bad day in a string of bad days, and "move forward" as quickly as possible.

When Bill died, I "dove in deep" as I always had, as that was what (I thought) helped me cope. But I realized executing my responsibilities as executor of his estate offered the perfect distraction—I could push through the pain without ever having to face it.

The exercise of lament could have been a huge blessing in those times. It would have afforded the opportunity to bring my body, mind and spirit in whatever state or "stage" they were in, and place all of it at the feet of God.

How freeing that could have been!

14

AN EXERCISE OF LAMENT

Digging into the nature of lament in some of the biblical texts that are foundational to my faith was a freeing (albeit tedious) exercise. I'm very thankful for the insights I gained. But when I concluded my research, I felt compelled to act—to take a first step in reaching out to God in a way I had perhaps never done before.

Regarding the death of my only brother to suicide, I don't believe I will ever "get over it"—not in my lifetime. It has changed me forever. And it would be absurd and insensitive to suggest that prayers of lament simply wash away our pain. What lament allows for is freedom—freedom from, as Karen Weeks states in her article, the risk of a hardened heart, pretending everything is fine.

I don't ever want to live that way.

What follows is my first attempt to write a prayer of lament. After burning much of a Saturday morning with meaningless tasks to avoid this endeavor, I finally plopped down at my desk and began writing—sort of. I edited my words as fast as I wrote them. It seemed impossible to allow my thoughts to bubble up from deep inside and flow onto the page.

A wise marketer once quipped, "Don't edit the brainstorm."

But I did precisely that. Honestly? I think I was afraid of what I might write.

After a couple weeks of thinking, writing, walking away in frustration, several periods of random weed-pulling in my back yard to delay the inevitable, and a surprising amount of tears, I finished my lament. I imagine I'll refer back to it in the days to come.

Dear God, my heavenly Father,

You created me, you saved me through faith.
You breathed your life into my soul.
You ordered the steps of my life and you walk with me
each day.

In spite of my humanity, my brokenness and my failings,
you embrace me with your loving kindness.

When I choose my path over yours,
you continue to keep me in your care
and wait patiently for me to come back to you.

Your mercies endure forever.

I know these truths about you deep inside me.
You paint so vivid a picture of your love
and sustaining grace on the canvas of my life.

Why is it so difficult to put my full faith and trust
in you?
I struggle to know you.

Though I know yours is the path I must follow to be
anchored in your truth,

An Exercise of Lament

there are days, years—decades—where the road is too difficult.

My journey is too much to bear, and I stray from you.

To endure—to thrive—I know I must seek you,
like a son who needs his father.

But far too often, rather than seek your face,
I turn inward and drown in a sea of worry.

You have blessed my life in so many ways, dear Lord.

Disease threatened my life. You brought healing and restoration.
You blessed me with two miracle daughters.

My marriage crumbled. Your strength sustained me.
You guided my steps as I sought to rebuild my life.

Yet, I doubt the truth of your words, and so easily forget
the fires through which you have walked by my side.

I forget the flames from which you've spared me.

Have mercy, dear Lord, for I come to you again,
thankful for your love and your welcoming arms,
yet carrying the weight of a burden like none I have ever known.

My only brother is dead—by his own hand.
The weight of so many questions crushes me.

Why would he do such a thing?
How could he do such a thing?

Why couldn't I help him?

Did he feel so trapped, so isolated that he turned inward, as I am so prone to do?

Did he turn from you and never look back?

I loved my brother but deep inside, I'm angry, dear Lord.
I'm angry and sad at the same time.

Heal my heart and mind, dear Lord.
Grant me peace in the midst of this pain.
Keep me close to you, in spite of my wandering.

You are my heavenly Father.

You created me, you saved me through faith.
You breathed your life into my soul.
You ordered the steps of my life and you walk with me each day.

You *will* draw me close to you and lead me out of this darkness.
You *will* make my way straight.
Because that is your nature, dear Lord.

May it be so.

Burn the truth of your word and your character into my heart and mind.
I will tell the story of your unceasing love.

Amen.

An Invitation

Now that I've shared my story, I want to shift the focus. What is troubling *you*? What is eating you alive from the inside out? Have you spent months—years—trying to "get over it" and keep "moving forward" as you or a loved one wrestles with crushing, life-altering circumstances?

Have you ever thought, "I'm done. I have nothing left. I'm spent."

If your answer to these questions is "Yes," then from the bottom of my heart I invite you to consider taking pen to paper and seizing this opportunity to write your own prayer of lament.

Each of us is on our own spiritual journey. And each of us views our lives and our world through different lenses. But one thing that unites us is our common humanity. We all ask the tough questions—who are we, why are we, why is life at times so incredibly difficult, and what are we to do with all of the questions, concerns and legitimate pain that churns up inside us?

I encourage you—wherever you are right now, today, in whatever state your body, mind and spirit are in—to reach into the deepest part of yourself (as deep as you feel you can go) and express your grief. Lament the anger, frustrations, nagging questions and injustices that are sucking the joy from your soul.

And if, over the course of your life you have enjoyed good times and rich blessings, I encourage you to allow your lament to acknowledge that as well. Express the joy and gratitude you feel over those things. But be aware—this exercise can be very difficult.

In my journey, there have been numerous occasions where I allowed my circumstances to cloud my ability to see the *good*—and there was plenty of it all around me. Even as I write this book, significant new medical challenges have me in their grip. But just like in the past, I'm surrounded by good and reminded of it each day. Some days more than others, I have to be intentional about recognizing and celebrating the *good*.

As much as I encourage you to express *your* joy, I encourage myself to do the same.

I've provided the following pages where you can write your lament, but use whatever tools feel most comfortable. Be as open and vulnerable as possible. Allow your words to flow, and try not to edit the brainstorm as I did. As much as you are able, allow your pain to come to the surface and spill out, onto the page. This may be an exercise that takes time to come to fruition. Allow yourself time.

MY LAMENT

..
..
..
..
..
..
..
..
..
..
..
..
..
..
..
..
..
..
..
..
..
..
..
..
..
..
..
..
..
..
..
..
..
..
..

15

FINAL THOUGHTS

I'm not sure "Final Thoughts" is the best or most appropriate title for the last chapter of this book. *Is there ever a last chapter in a story such as this?* When I sat down to write it, I quickly realized I had no "final" thoughts—only thoughts.

I imagine that will be the case for the rest of my life. Since Bill passed in 2016, there have been so many occasions where I've wanted to call him just to talk and have some laughs.

I wish Bill could come up to my neck of the woods in Northern California for a walk on the Sundial Bridge in Redding or a drive up to Mt. Shasta, just to stand with him and stare at it in wonder, like we used to do on our hiking trips.

Perhaps as more time passes, and with God's grace, the times where my thoughts lead only to frustration and sadness over Bill being gone will become less frequent; tapping into the gift of lament will surely play a role in that process.

I look forward to a time when the fond memories I have of my brother and the good times we shared leave a stronger imprint on my heart than does the pain of losing him.

APPENDIX
A STUDY OF LAMENT IN THE OLD TESTAMENT OF THE BIBLE

The American Heritage Dictionary defines *lament* as both a verb and noun.

As a transitive verb, it is...

1. To express grief for or about; mourn...
2. To regret deeply; deplore...

As an intransitive verb, it is...

1. To grieve audibly; wail.
2. To express sorrow or regret.

What lament *isn't* is whining or complaining.

Rather, it is the fullest, deepest and perhaps most genuine expression of grief. In the Bible, two books in the Old Testament —Psalms and Lamentations—are devoted in large part to the expression of grief and mourning. The latter of the two books is devoted entirely to the subject.

The book of Psalms is the longest in the Bible. Contained within its pages are 150 psalms (or hymns) that address a wide range of subjects. There are psalms the Nation of Israel would

Appendix

sing to lift corporate praises to God, and others an individual would sing to express personal thanksgiving.

Other psalms speak of the city of Jerusalem and its theological relevance to the Israelites—as "Zion," their spiritual stronghold—rather than its geographical or geopolitical significance.

Another group of songs, known as "royal" psalms, were sung to address the kings who ruled Israel; all were from the line of David and considered sons of God upon their ascension to the throne. The kings were responsible for oversight of all aspects of Israelite life. These psalms were sung at royal weddings, before battles, after conquests, during times of chaos and times of triumph, by individuals, in some instances, or by the entire Nation.

Then there are the psalms of lament—songs of personal pain where the "misery of life's misfortunes, the desperation of human distress, the anguish of personal adversity, and the agony of mortal affliction [come] to expression...."[1] Of the 150 psalms contained within the book of Psalms, 60 are considered songs of lament.

Each type of psalm served an important purpose in the lives of the ancient Israelites. The psalms were part of the fabric of the culture, integral to their faith and never treated as an adornment.

When it came to the practice of *lament*, the psalms of lament were an essential step in the healing process, regardless of the source of anguish. Though there is some deviation within the collection of the lament psalms, most share a common, intentional structure. Some biblical scholars have identified as few as three or four distinct sections in the structure, while others, including Dr. John Hayes, have identified as many as seven.

Here are the seven sections Hayes delineates that form the structure of the psalms of lament:

1. Address to God

2. Description of Distress
3. Plea for Redemption
4. Statement of Confidence
5. Confession of Sin or Affirmation of Innocence
6. Pledge or Vow
7. Conclusion[2]

Some psalms lament illness or sickness.

Psalm 6 is one such lament. The psalmist is in the midst of personal, physical suffering. He begins his lament with a cry for God's mercy. He laments his weakness, his "troubled bones" and a troubled soul, and paints a vivid picture of a man so distraught as to leave his bed and couch soaked by the volume of his tears.

> ^{1}*O Lord, do not rebuke me in Your anger,*
> *Nor chasten me in Your hot displeasure.*
> ^{2}*Have mercy on me, O Lord, for I am weak;*
> *O Lord, heal me, for my bones are troubled.*
> ^{3}*My soul also is greatly troubled;*
> *But You, O Lord—how long?*
> ^{4}*Return, O Lord, deliver me!*
> *Oh, save me for Your mercies' sake!*
> ^{5}*For in death there is no remembrance of You;*
> *In the grave who will give You thanks?*
> ^{6}*I am weary with my groaning;*
> *All night I make my bed swim;*
> *I drench my couch with my tears.*
> ^{7}*My eye wastes away because of grief;*
> *It grows old because of all my enemies.*
>
> — PSALM 6:1-7

From the text, it appears the man's physical suffering came at the hands of others—called "workers of iniquity" in the eighth

Appendix

verse. Neither the identity of the persons or the nature of their deeds is disclosed.

After praying for relief from the influence of the evil men, the psalmist makes a bold declaration of faith that God has heard his petitions. He then prays essentially a curse "that justice will take the form of an affliction similar to what he has suffered."[3] The psalmist finds hope through his confidence that God's justice will be brought against evil and His mercy poured out upon the psalmist.

> [8]*Depart from me, all you workers of iniquity;*
> *For the Lord has heard the voice of my weeping.*
> [9]*The Lord has heard my supplication;*
> *The Lord will receive my prayer.*
> [10]*Let all my enemies be ashamed and greatly troubled;*
> *Let them turn back and be ashamed suddenly.*
>
> — PSALM 6:8-10

Some psalms lament accusations.

Psalm 7 is an example of this type of lament. The psalmist first declares his trust in God and pleads his innocence. Then, in an oath of sorts—a "conditional self-curse,"[4] he declares his innocence but prays that if he is found guilty, the punishment due him would come at the hands of his accusers.

> [1]*Lord my God, in You I put my trust;*
> *Save me from all those who persecute me;*
> *And deliver me,*
> [2]*Lest they tear me like a lion,*
> *Rending me in pieces, while there is none to deliver.*
> [3]*O Lord my God, if I have done this:*
> *If there is iniquity in my hands,*
> [4]*If I have repaid evil to him who was at peace with me,*
> *Or have plundered my enemy without cause,*

Appendix

> ^{5}*Let the enemy pursue me and overtake me;*
> *Yes, let him trample my life to the earth,*
> *And lay my honor in the dust.* Selah
>
> — PSALM 7:1-5

Believing that God sees his cause as just, the psalmist calls on God to bring about His righteous intervention and vindication from the accusations of his enemies. The lament continues as God is declared to be a just judge of the wicked. The psalmist laments the depth of wickedness, from its initial inception to its outworking through wicked deeds.

> ^{6}*Arise, O Lord, in Your anger;*
> *Lift Yourself up because of the rage of my enemies;*
> *Rise up for me to the judgment You have commanded!*
> ^{7}*So the congregation of the peoples shall surround You;*
> *For their sakes, therefore, return on high.*
> ^{8}*The Lord shall judge the peoples;*
> *Judge me, O Lord, according to my righteousness,*
> *And according to my integrity within me.*
>
> ^{9}*Oh, let the wickedness of the wicked come to an end,*
> *But establish the just;*
> *For the righteous God tests the hearts and minds.*
> ^{10}*My defense is of God,*
> *Who saves the upright in heart.*
> ^{11}*God is a just judge,*
> *And God is angry with the wicked every day.*
> ^{12}*If he does not turn back,*
> *He will sharpen His sword;*
> *He bends His bow and makes it ready.*
> ^{13}*He also prepares for Himself instruments of death;*
> *He makes His arrows into fiery shafts.*

> ^{14}Behold, the wicked brings forth iniquity;
> Yes, he conceives trouble and brings forth falsehood.
> ^{15}He made a pit and dug it out,
> And has fallen into the ditch which he made.
> ^{16}His trouble shall return upon his own head,
> And his violent dealing shall come down on his own crown.
>
> — PSALM 7:6-16

After affirming God's righteousness, the lament concludes with a declaration of praise. The psalmist "[ends] this psalm—which began in gloom—on a high note of praise. He could praise, because he took his cause to God and in faith left it there."[5]

> I will praise the Lord according to His righteousness,
> And will sing praise to the name of the Lord Most High.
>
> — PSALM 7:17

Some psalms lament oppression.

Psalm 140 exemplifies this type of lament. A plea to God for *deliverance* begins the prayer. The psalmist then paints a vivid and compelling picture of the nature of the oppression—evil, violent men who plan evil things, whose tongues are like snakes and whose lips conceal their venom.

> ^{1}Deliver me, O Lord, from evil men;
> Preserve me from violent men,
> ^{2}Who plan evil things in their hearts;
> They continually gather together for war.
> ^{3}They sharpen their tongues like a serpent;
> The poison of asps is under their lips. Selah

Appendix

— PSALM 140:1-3

The lament continues with a second plea to God, this time for *preservation*. The psalmist provides further descriptions of both the intentions and actions the evil men have taken against him.

> [4]*Keep me, O Lord, from the hands of the wicked;*
> *Preserve me from violent men,*
> *Who have purposed to make my steps stumble.*
> [5]*The proud have hidden a snare for me, and cords;*
> *They have spread a net by the wayside;*
> *They have set traps for me. Selah*
>
> — PSALM 140:4,5

After bringing his cause before the Lord and asking for his help, the psalmist makes a strong declaration of faith and includes a new plea—for God's *justice* to intervene and come against the evil the psalmist laments.

> [6]*I said to the Lord: "You are my God;*
> *Hear the voice of my supplications, O Lord.*
> [7]*O God the Lord, the strength of my salvation,*
> *You have covered my head in the day of battle.*
> [8]*Do not grant, O Lord, the desires of the wicked;*
> *Do not further his wicked scheme,*
> *Lest they be exalted. Selah*
>
> — PSALM 140:6-8

In the next phase of the lament, the psalmist prays a curse against his oppressors, in which the depth and rawness of his emotions are expressed. Where some of the psalms of lament use

Appendix

less impassioned language in their pleas to God, the majority of them employ "vitriolic and caustic language...."[6]

> [9]"*As for the head of those who surround me,*
> *Let the evil of their lips cover them;*
> [10]*Let burning coals fall upon them;*
> *Let them be cast into the fire,*
> *Into deep pits, that they rise not up again.*
> [11]*Let not a slanderer be established in the earth;*
> *Let evil hunt the violent man to overthrow him.*"
>
> — PSALM 140:9-11

When such laments are read today, the language can seem unreasonable, jarring and "over the top." The scratching of one's head over *why* may be alleviated by two points worth considering.

First, the laments of the psalmist may employ this toxic level of vitriol to paint an almost overly vivid picture of the oppression, as the justice they seek from God "must be equal not only to the adversity suffered by the lamenting party but also to the enemies' real or imagined wishes and desires for the oppressed."[7]

Second, the expression of raw emotion where the psalmist holds nothing back, allows for complete emotional expression—and a potentially cathartic experience; his seemingly "unhinged" rants may spare him from a lifetime of deep psychological problems.

In the concluding verses of Psalm 140, the psalmist proclaims his faith in God—the God who will always care for the afflicted and poor. As is the case in the majority of the psalms of lament, what began in sadness concludes in confident joy.

> [12]*I know that the Lord will maintain*
> *The cause of the afflicted,*

Appendix

> *And justice for the poor.*
> *¹³Surely the righteous shall give thanks to Your name;*
> *The upright shall dwell in Your presence.*
>
> — PSALM 140:12,13

Some of the psalms of lament address sin and repentance.

Of the 60 psalms of lament, seven are considered "penitential" psalms as they lament the issue of personal sin. Psalm 51 may be the most familiar of the penitential psalms. One of the reasons for this is its compelling backstory.

When reading the Bible's books of the Old Testament, it can be quite easy to feel overwhelmed. The often tedious nature of the content—seemingly endless genealogies of kings, exhaustive laws and the somber warnings of the prophets (and sometimes the little voice in the back of your head, whispering, "who cares?")—can prompt a person to wonder why they even considered perusing such content.

Over the years that thought has most definitely occupied space inside my head.

It's understandable how someone could walk away, shake their head and dismiss the texts (especially the Old Testament) as the most boring and overwhelmingly confusing content they've ever encountered.

For those who have ever felt this way (writing to myself here as well), the backstory behind King David's lament in Psalm 51 offers compelling evidence to the contrary. Pastor Eric Stillman paints a vivid picture of the historical context.

> "David has been a very successful king over Israel—slayer of Goliath, man after God's heart, writer of the Psalms. But in his success, he is growing spiritually complacent and lazy. In 2 Samuel 11, David has decided to stay home when he should have been out leading his troops in battle. As he is strolling on the roof of his palace, David sees a woman named Bathsheba

Appendix

bathing. Bathsheba is the wife of Uriah, one of his most loyal fighting men. But David is overcome with lust, and so he sends for her, sleeps with her, and impregnates her. He tries to cover it up by bringing Uriah home to sleep with his wife, but Uriah refuses. And so, David sends Uriah back to battle, and instructs the general to have Uriah killed in battle. And then David takes Bathsheba to be his wife.

David thinks he has gotten away with this, but he has not. God sends Nathan the prophet to confront him about what he has done. As David confesses what he has done, God spares David's life, but the son he and Bathsheba have conceived will die. And this experience becomes a major turning point in David's life. After this sin, David's life is filled with heartache. Soon afterwards, David's son Amnon rapes his half-sister, Tamar. Another son, Absalom, in response, murders Amnon. Over time, Absalom steals the hearts of the people away from David and conspires to take the throne from his father. David has to flee for his life and only returns to the throne when Absalom is killed.

Just think about the chain of events that was put into motion by David's sinful decision not to be with his army, where he was supposed to be: rape, incest, murder, suicide, betrayal, insurrection, war, and exile. Do you think David would have gone back and done it differently if he could have?"[8]

The issues in play here are some of the nastiest schemes man can perpetrate against his fellow man. Though these events occurred thousands of years ago, the story could have been written today, and I suspect, embraced by a sizable audience, thirsty for its themes.

In Psalm 51, King David expresses a prayer of repentance following a powerful encounter with the prophet Nathan, who confronted David about his sins. The narrative of *that* confrontation is found in the book of 2 Samuel, chapter 12.

In the first half of the psalm (verses 1-12), David's lament begins with a plea for God's mercy. He "admits his transgressions and acknowledges the appropriateness of God's judgment."[9] His plea is grounded in his knowledge of God's loving kindness and bountiful mercy. He asks that God act—blot out, wash and cleanse—the sin he has committed, as he is acutely aware of his sinful condition.

> *[1]Have mercy upon me, O God,*
> *According to Your loving kindness;*
> *According to the multitude of Your tender mercies,*
> *Blot out my transgressions.*
> *[2]Wash me thoroughly from my iniquity,*
> *And cleanse me from my sin.*
>
> *[3]For I acknowledge my transgressions,*
> *And my sin is always before me.*
> *[4]Against You, You only, have I sinned,*
> *And done this evil in Your sight—*
> *That You may be found just when You speak,*
> *And blameless when You judge.*
>
> *[5]Behold, I was brought forth in iniquity,*
> *And in sin my mother conceived me.*
> *6 Behold, You desire truth in the inward parts,*
> *And in the hidden part You will make me to know*
>   *wisdom.*
>
> — PSALM 51:1-6

As David's lament continues, he repeats his request that God act—purge and wash him—so he will be without blemish in God's eyes. David bangs on the gates of Heaven, confident

Appendix

God will be merciful to him as he acknowledges his sinful state. His lament longs for God to bring about a total transformation.

His deepest desire—to the depth of his bones—is for his brokenness to become joy, gladness and rejoicing.

> *7Purge me with hyssop, and I shall be clean;*
> *Wash me, and I shall be whiter than snow.*
> *8Make me hear joy and gladness,*
> *That the bones You have broken may rejoice.*
> *9Hide Your face from my sins,*
> *And blot out all my iniquities.*
>
> *10Create in me a clean heart, O God,*
> *And renew a steadfast spirit within me.*
> *11Do not cast me away from Your presence,*
> *And do not take Your Holy Spirit from me.*
>
> *12Restore to me the joy of Your salvation,*
> *And uphold me by Your generous Spirit.*
>
> — PSALM 51:7-12

In the second half of the psalm (verses 13-19), the nature of the lament shifts from David's penitent pleas for God's forgiveness and restoration, to a joyful humility. His prayer in this section includes several specific promises to declare how he "would manifest his sense of the divine mercy if he was forgiven: expressing the purpose to lead a new life; to devote himself to the duties of religion; to do all in his power to repair the evils of his conduct, and especially to induce others to avoid the way of sin, warning them by his example."[10]

If God would restore him, David vows to teach sinners the ways of God (verse 13). If God would deliver David from his guilt (over ordering Uriah to be killed in battle), David vows to

Appendix

sing of God's righteousness and offer up praises to Him (verses 14, 15).

What follows in the next two verses is a confident assertion by the psalmist. Rather than sacrifices and burnt offerings—essential components of the Law God instituted for ancient Israel—David states what pleases the heart of God more than rote (impersonal?) ritual, is when his people come to Him in their brokenness with a contrite heart.

Though David affirms his respect for God's Law in this second half of the psalm, he has confidence God will not reject those who approach Him in this most personal manner.

> [13] *Then I will teach transgressors Your ways,*
> *And sinners shall be converted to You.*
> [14] *Deliver me from the guilt of bloodshed, O God,*
> *The God of my salvation,*
> *And my tongue shall sing aloud of Your righteousness.*
> [15] *O Lord, open my lips,*
> *And my mouth shall show forth Your praise.*
> [16] *For You do not desire sacrifice, or else I would give it;*
> *You do not delight in burnt offering.*
> [17] *The sacrifices of God are a broken spirit,*
> *A broken and a contrite heart—*
> *These, O God, You will not despise.*
>
> — PSALM 51:13-17

In the final two verses of David's lament, he pleads "that God would interpose and bless Zion,"[11] (possibly a reference to the actual city of Jerusalem), "that the great work might be completed in which he had been engaged in defending the city, and in preparing a place which would be secure, where God might be worshipped, and where sacrifices and offerings might perpetually ascend on his altar."[12]

Another possible explanation of the lament's reference to

Appendix

"Zion" is that David refers to Jerusalem as a metaphor for himself and his need for God to bring complete restoration to David's own spiritual house.

> *¹⁸Do good in Your good pleasure to Zion;*
> *Build the walls of Jerusalem.*
> *¹⁹Then You shall be pleased with the sacrifices of*
>   *righteousness,*
> *With burnt offering and whole burnt offering;*
> *Then they shall offer bulls on Your altar.*
>
> — PSALM 51:18-19

What this psalm of lament brings to light is David's *intentional* process of repentance of sin to bring restoration to his personal spiritual house. He knows doing so will allow him to thrive under the blessings of God's loving kindness, tender mercies, justice, blamelessness, wisdom, salvation and generous spirit.

Writing about the open, honest and unrestrained language in the psalms of lament, the late Reverend John Endres offers the following encouragement.

> "The verbs and adjectives with which they describe and address God model for us open, honest biblical prayer of lamentation. They help us to learn *how* to articulate the pain and the grief that we experience; we do not have to internalize it all, let it fester, grow sour. Laments lower the risk of venting anger in dangerous and inappropriate ways. When we can pray laments we acknowledge God's covenantal bond with us. Could we ever address a mere acquaintance or associate so directly, without fear of reprisal, of total abandonment? At times I wonder if we can afford not to pray psalms of lament in our day."[13]

But wait, there's more.

Appendix

Similar to the book of Psalms, the book of Lamentations, whose authorship is ascribed by many biblical scholars to the prophet Jeremiah, is a second book in the Old Testament that illustrates the significance of lament in the lives of the ancient Israelites.

The book is a collection of five poems that mourn the destruction of the city of Jerusalem in 586 B.C. Nearly two years prior, the army of the Babylonian empire led by King Nebuchadnezzar had launched a siege of the city and left a path of gut-wrenching destruction in its wake.

With the exception of some who were kept in the land by their conquerers to provide agricultural slave labor, the majority of people who inhabited Jerusalem and the surrounding region were gathered up and sent into exile in Babylonia.

The book of Lamentations is a funeral dirge about the death of the city of Jerusalem.

Much like the psalms of lament in the book of Psalms, the five poems in Lamentations offer a vivid example of the depth of grief and mourning by the prophet. Forty years prior to the city's destruction, Jeremiah had been called by God to warn the people of the consequences that would come upon them for their unrepentant sin.

Over the forty years Jeremiah prophesied of the coming judgment, he endured unrelenting persecution; the Israelites never heeded his warnings. In Lamentations, Jeremiah acknowledges the destruction of the city as "a tragedy entirely of Jerusalem's making. The people of this once great city experienced the judgment of the holy God, and the results were devastating."[14]

> [5]*Her adversaries have become the master,*
> *Her enemies prosper;*
> *For the Lord has afflicted her*
> *Because of the multitude of her transgressions.*

Appendix

> Her children have gone into captivity before the enemy.
>
> ⁹Her uncleanness is in her skirts;
> She did not consider her destiny;
> Therefore her collapse was awesome;
> She had no comforter.
> "O Lord, behold my affliction,
> For the enemy is exalted!"
>
> ¹²"Is it nothing to you, all you who pass by?
> Behold and see
> If there is any sorrow like my sorrow,
> Which has been brought on me,
> Which the Lord has inflicted
> In the day of His fierce anger.
>
> — LAMENTATIONS 1:5, 9, 12

The five poems contained in the book of Lamentations utilize an intentional structure like the laments in the book of Psalms. But in Lamentations, the first four poems employ a completely different structure known as an *acrostic*. This is a poem "in which the initial letters of each successive line form a word, phrase or pattern."[15]

One type of acrostic structure is used in the first two chapters of the book. The first line in each block (or stanza) of three verses begins with the 22 consecutive letters of the Hebrew alphabet.

Chapter 3 deviates from this acrostic structure, in that its 66 verses are grouped into 22 three-verse blocks where all three lines in each block begin with the same letter of the Hebrew alphabet and continues in consecutive alphabetic order through the end of the chapter.

Chapter 4 is similar in structure to the first two chapters, but the verses are grouped into blocks of two lines rather than three.

The book of Lamentations concludes with the fifth chapter.

Appendix

Unlike the previous four, Chapter 5 is a prayer rather than another dirge.

After four chapters lamenting the destruction of the city of Jerusalem in graphic detail (and from several points of view), the subject of the lament in Chapter 5 shifts to the *consequences* of the devastation that has come to the Nation of Israel.

Every aspect of the Israelite's lives has been deeply affected by the destruction and occupation by the Babylonians. Chapter 5 lays bare the full impact of God's judgment brought against His people for their sin and rebellion against His commandments.

The first 18 verses of the chapter lament the overwhelming scope of their loss: their material possessions, homes and family members, their impoverished state, the weight of their sin, the upheaval of the social order, the ever-present risk of death, the famine which has spread throughout the land, the unspeakable horrors committed against every segment of the population, the loss of all sense of community and the joy of their hearts turned to mourning.

The last four verses of the chapter conclude the lament with an "appeal to the compassion of God so as to gain His help,"[16] and His restoration of the Nation.

> *[19]You, O Lord, remain forever;*
> *Your throne from generation to generation.*
> *[20]Why do You forget us forever,*
> *And forsake us for so long a time?*
> *[21]Turn us back to You, O Lord, and we will be restored;*
> *Renew our days as of old,*
> *[22]Unless You have utterly rejected us,*
> *And are very angry with us!*
>
> — LAMENTATIONS 5:19-22

As we endure seasons of pain and suffering in our lives and bear witness to it on a grander scale throughout our world, we

Appendix

can lean into the sentiment of Lamentations 5, and draw strength from it.

The lament texts of the Old Testament communicate several truths that can help us through our own seasons of pain.

Lament affords an opportunity to take healthy, appropriate action in the midst of dire circumstances. The model of the five stages of grief is a tool that allows us to get a sense—a snapshot—of our attitudes, feelings and thoughts at any point in a journey of pain. But once informed using that framework, what are we to do with that knowledge?

Knowledge (information) is helpful but not a *solution* to our pain. In contrast, lament is a tool with which we can turn *awareness* into *action* by articulating our grief.

Lament is an intentional process. There is no quick, "band aid" solution to the problem of pain. In the book of Psalms, the 60 songs of lament utilized a structure that consisted of perhaps as many as seven separate elements. In Lamentations, Jeremiah's grief over the death of the city of Jerusalem was fully expressed over five poems, each written from a different point of view using ordered and intentional structures.

We are all individuals. The content of our grief (our lament) and how we grieve is unique to each of us. But being intentional in addressing our grief and allowing a process for it helps ensure its full expression—over time.

Lament makes room for *hope*. The psalmists initially engaged God at the height of their despair. And though the illnesses, accusations, oppressions or remorse over their sins may have continued for a time, the overwhelming majority of their laments concluded in confident hope of resolution and restoration by

God. In the songs of lament sung by the Israelites, the people poured out their hearts to God and asked Him "to answer according to His unfailing love because He [was] a God of justice and righteousness, and because He [had] been faithful in the past."[17]

Through lament, the Israelites were able to recall their history with God and the blessings He had bestowed upon them; that allowed hope to permeate the fabric of their grief.

We can do the same.

NOTES

9. Looking Back

1. Fatima Nasrallah, "What Does Concussion Do To the Brain," Queensland Brain Institute, accessed January 18, 2023, https://qbi.uq.edu.au/blog/2018/05/what-does-concussion-do-brain.
2. "The Seriousness of Concussions and TBI," Amen Clinics, accessed October 24, 2022,
   https://www.amenclinics.com/blog/must-take-concussions-seriously/.
3. "Concussion," Cleveland Clinic, accessed January 18, 2023, https://my.clevelandclinic.org/health/diseases/15038-concussion.

11. Trying To Make Sense of It All

1. "Suicidal Thoughts & Behavior," Amen Clinics, accessed October 24, 2022, https://www.amenclinics.com/conditions/suicidal-thoughts-and-behavior/.
2. "Risk factors, Protective Factors, and Warning Signs," American Foundation for Suicide Prevention, accessed April 27, 2022,
   https://afsp.org/risk-factors-protective-factors-and-warning-signs.
3. "Risk factors, Protective Factors, and Warning Signs."
4. "5 Stages of Grief and Loss," Jonas Hill Hospital and Clinics, accessed May 30, 2022, https://jonashill.org/5-stages-of-grief-and-loss/.

13. Realizations

1. Karen Weeks, "Lament: A Path to Healing," Desert Streams, accessed March 13, 2022,
   https://desertstreams.org/lament-a-path-to-healing.

Appendix

1. John H. Hayes, *Understanding the Psalms* (Valley Forge, PA: Judson Press, 1976), 57.
2. Hayes, *Understanding the Psalms*, 58.
3. Kyle Ronchetto, "Lamenting a Wasting Disease: A Commentary on Psalm 6," DigitalCommons@Macalester College, accessed April 8, 2022,
   https://digitalcommons.macalester.edu/classicsjournal/vol4/iss1/1.
4. Hayes, *Understanding the Psalms*, 71

Notes

5. David Guzik, "Psalm 7 – Confidence in God's Deliverance," Enduring Word, accessed April 7, 2022, https://enduringword.com/bible-commentary/psalm-7/.
6. Hayes, *Understanding the Psalms*, 79
7. Hayes, *Understanding the Psalms*, 79
8. Eric Stillman, "Lamenting Our Sin," New Life Christian Fellowship, accessed April 14, 2022, https://www.newlife-ct.org/sermons/sermon/2020-06-07/lamenting-our-sin.
9. Hayes, *Understanding the Psalms*, 83
10. Albert Barnes, "Commentary on Psalms 51." "Barnes' Notes on the Whole Bible," StudyLight.org, accessed April 18, 2022, https://www.studylight.org/commentaries/eng/bnb/psalms-51.html.
11. Barnes, Commentary on Psalms 51.
12. Barnes, Commentary on Psalms 51.
13. John Endres, "Cry Out to God in Our Need—Psalms of Lament," Santa Clara University, accessed June 11, 2022, https://www.scu.edu/media/jst/resources/Endres-lament-the-way.pdf.
14. Chuck Swindoll, "Lamentations," The Bible-Teaching Ministry of Pastor Chuck Swindoll, accessed April 22, 2022, https://insight.org/resources/bible/the-major-prophets/lamentations.
15. M. Bruce and M.D. Coogan, *Oxford Companion to the Bible* (Oxford: University Press, 1999), 6.
16. James E. Smith, "An Exegetical Commentary on Lamentations," International College of the Bible, accessed April 21, https://icotb.org/resources/Lamentations.pdf.
17. Glenn Packiam, "Five Things to Know About Lament," N.T. Wright Online, accessed March 11, 2022, https://www.ntwrightonline.org/five-things-to-know-about-lament.

BIBLIOGRAPHY

Amen Clinics. "The Seriousness of Concussions and TBI." Accessed October 24, 2022.
https://www.amenclinics.com/blog/must-take-concussions-seriously/.

American Foundation for Suicide Prevention. "Risk factors, protective factors, and warning signs." Accessed April 27, 2022.
https://afsp.org/risk-factors-protective-factors-and-warning-signs.

Barnes, A. "Commentary on Psalms 51." "Barnes' Notes on the Whole Bible." Accessed April 18, 2022.
https://www.studylight.org/commentaries/eng/bnb/psalms-51.html. 1870

Bruce, M. and M.D. Coogan. *Oxford Companion to the Bible*. Oxford: University Press, 1999.

Bullock, C. Hassell. *An Introduction to the Old Testament Poetic Books*. Chicago: Moody Press, 1979.

Carlson, Dwight and Susan Carlson Wood. *When Life Isn't Fair*. Eugene: Harvest House Publishers, 1989.

Cleveland Clinic. "Concussion," Accessed January 18, 2023.
https://my.clevelandclinic.org/health/diseases/15038-concussion.

Endres, John. "Cry Out to God in Our Need—Psalms of Lament." Accessed June 11, 2022.
https://www.scu.edu/media/jst/resources/Endres-lament-the-way.pdf.

Guzik, David. "Psalm 7 – Confidence in God's Deliverance." Accessed April 7, 2022.
https://enduringword.com/bible-commentary/psalm-7/.

Hayes, John H. *Understanding the Psalms*. Valley Forge: Judson Press, 1976.

Jonas Hill Hospital and Clinics. "5 Stages of Grief and Loss." Accessed May 30, 2022.

Bibliography

https://jonashill.org/5-stages-of-grief-and-loss/.

Lewis, C. S. *The Problem of Pain*. New York: Macmillan Publishing Company, 1962.

Nasrallah, Fatima. "What Does Concussion Do To the Brain," Accessed January 18, 2023.
https://qbi.uq.edu.au/blog/2018/05/what-does-concussion-do-brain.

Packiam Glenn. "Five Things to Know About Lament." Accessed March 11, 2022.
https://www.ntwrightonline.org/five-things-to-know-about-lament.

Ronchetto, Kyle. "Lamenting a Wasting Disease: A Commentary on Psalm 6," Studies in Mediterranean Antiquity and Classics: Vol. 4: Iss. 1, Article 1, Accessed April 8, 2022.

Smith, James E. "An Exegetical Commentary on Lamentations." Accessed April 21, 2022.
https://icotb.org/resources/Lamentations.pdf.

Stillman, Eric. "Lamenting Our Sin." Accessed April 14, 2022.
https://www.newlife-ct.org/sermons/sermon/2020-06-07/lamenting-our-sin.

Swindoll, Chuck. "Lamentations" Accessed April 22, 2022.
https://insight.org/resources/bible/the-major-prophets/lamentations.

Weeks Karen. "Lament: A Path to Healing." Accessed March 13, 2022.
https://desertstreams.org/lament-a-path-to-healing.

RESOURCES

Suicide Awareness and Prevention

American Foundation for Suicide Prevention
https://afsp.org/suicide-prevention-resources

Call or text 988 or Text TALK to 741741

Centers for Disease Control and Prevention
https://www.cdc.gov/suicide/resources/index.html

From the CDC Website:
Contact the 988 Suicide and Crisis Lifeline if you are experiencing mental health-related distress or are worried about a loved one who may need crisis support.

Call or text 988
Chat at 988lifeline.org

Connect with a trained crisis counselor. 988 is confidential, free, and available 24/7/365.

Visit the 988 Suicide and Crisis Lifeline for more information at 988lifeline.org

National Action Alliance for Suicide Prevention
https://theactionalliance.org/

For Veterans and Military Suicide Prevention Resources:
https://theactionalliance.org/veteran-and-military-suicide-prevention-resources

Suicide Awareness Voices of Education
https://save.org/

For International Resources:

Resources

https://save.org/find-help/international-resources/

The JED Foundation
https://jedfoundation.org/

From the JED Foundation Website:
"JED empowers teens and young adults by building resiliency and life skills, promoting social connectedness, and encouraging help-seeking and help-giving behaviors through our nationally recognized programs, digital channels, and partnerships, as well as through the media. JED strengthens schools by working directly with high schools, colleges, and universities—representing millions of students—to put systems, programs, and policies in place to create a culture of caring that protects student mental health, builds life skills, and makes it more likely that struggling students will seek help and be recognized, connected to care, and supported. We mobilize communities by providing education, training, and tools to families, friends, media, and others."

The Suicide Solution
By Dr. Daniel Emina & Rick Lawrence
Published by Salem Books
Available at Amazon.com

From the book's Amazon.com listing:
"This is a book for people who are struggling to find their way out of a cave of anxiety, depression, and suicidal thoughts—and for anyone who cares for someone who's been lost in that cave.

Suicide is now the leading cause of death among young adults 18-34, and the fourth-leading cause of death among the middle-aged.

Just as a computer's hardware determines its foundational capabilities and its software determines how it interfaces with the world, humans' hardware is tied to our biology and our software dictates how we relate to others and ourselves. Together, these parts of our identity determine our functionality, limitations, and possibilities.

We *become* the story we have decided to live inside. When Jesus said, "I have come to set captives free," He meant that He came to "de-bug" our programming. Jesus invites us to partner with Him to bring to the surface and then move past our debilitating bugs.

This book is a conversation between a minister and a psychiatrist. Informed by the clinical realities of anxiety, depression, and suicide, the authors draw from the transformational relational strategies of Jesus to chart a path into life and freedom."

Traumatic Brain Injury

Amen Clinics
https://www.amenclinics.com/

From the Amen Clinics Website:
"Our brain imaging work clearly shows that we are not dealing with mental health issues, rather we are dealing with brain health issues that steal your mind. At Amen Clinics, we believe that brain health is the foundation of overall health, well-being, and success. When the brain is healthy, people are happier, physically healthier, wealthier, and they make better decisions, which helps them be more successful in every area of life. When the brain is not healthy, for whatever reason, people are sadder, sicker, poorer, and their decision-making suffers, which diminishes their chances for getting what they want out of life.

Unlike traditional psychiatry that rarely looks at the organ it treats, we use brain SPECT imaging, which measures blood flow and activity in the brain to help us more accurately diagnose and treat your needs. Our comprehensive evaluations also include laboratory testing (when necessary), clinical assessments, your personal history, and more. This helps us provide you with a comprehensive, personalized treatment plan utilizing the least toxic, most effective solutions to enhance brain health.

Achieving our mission to boost brain health not only helps individuals prevent or alleviate suffering, but it also helps everyone around them—family members, friends, and coworkers. In addition, helping one person's brain can create a lasting legacy that will empower and improve the lives of their future generations.

Our unique, well-researched process results in higher than average success rates. In fact, we perform outcome studies on our patients, which have found that 85% of people report a better quality of life after treatment at Amen Clinics.

Resources

The most important lesson we have learned from over 200,000 brain scans is that you are NOT stuck with the brain you have. You can change your brain and change your life. And we can help you do it."

Cleveland Clinic
https://my.clevelandclinic.org/health/diseases/8874-traumatic-brain-injury

Johns Hopkins Medical
https://www.hopkinsmedicine.org/health/conditions-and-diseases/traumatic-brain-injury

Mayo Clinic
https://www.mayoclinic.org/diseases-conditions/traumatic-brain-injury/symptoms-causes/syc-20378557

Stanford Healthcare
https://stanfordhealthcare.org/medical-conditions/brain-and-nerves/traumatic-brain-injury.html

ACKNOWLEDGMENTS

I'm beyond grateful for the following dear folks who supported me in the aftermath of my brother's death and helped me negotiate numerous detours, road blocks and speed bumps in the process of writing this book:

Dick and Becky Ashley—for help with the heavy lifting in San Francisco, and for providing a loving and caring forever home for a needy Honda Accord.

Matt Bohlin—for being my brother from another mother, a great friend, and a huge help during Operation "Clean Sweep" in San Francisco. I'd convoy with you anytime.

Tony and Judy Bohlin—for your support and encouragement, and for allowing your front porch to become a staging area for the perpetual yard sale.

Gordon Borneman—for our enduring friendship and your help during one of the most terrible seasons of my life.

Rich Bullock—for our friendship, your enthusiasm for this project, and your excellent editorial and formatting skills.

Dr. Earl Henslin—for our conversations about this project, your wisdom and wise counsel, and for our connection in the branches of the family tree.

Dr. Gordon Ho Wan Li, my Brain Surgeon, and the nursing staff at Stanford University Medical Center, Palo Alto, CA—for the excellent skills you brought to bear, and the compassionate care I received.

The Providers and staff at Good Samaritan Hospital Inpatient Rehab Facility, Los Gatos, CA—for helping me get back on my feet after brain surgery, for making rehab fun and rewarding, and for your enthusiasm and encouragement to keep getting stronger so I could finish this book.

My Radiation Oncologist, Dr. Matthew Allen and staff at Valor Oncology, Redding, CA—for helping me fight my second brain tumor battle. You guys provided excellent care, lots of laughs, and perhaps the best six weeks of music appreciation banter ever.

Jim Randolph—for our friendship, your prayers and encouragement, your scholarly insights into the texts of the Old Testament, and our shared appreciation for a tall, frosty—tasteless and odorless—Iocane. We would know it anywhere.

The late Cory Severud—for our many conversations about facing life's most terrible challenges, the example you were to me as you chose to live, laugh and smile as you waged your courageous battle against the dragon, and for convincing me to finish writing this book. May you rest in peace among the angels.

Roberta Veit—for the insights and wisdom you have imparted to me throughout our long friendship and for inspiring me to dig deep into the nature of lament.

ABOUT THE AUTHOR

Rob Henslin is an award-winning graphic designer and marketing communications professional—and an enthusiastic writer. He's passionate about finding ways to make the most of the hardships he has endured so he can help others through difficult times. He has volunteered his time to assist the Be The Match bone marrow registry (marrow.org) and has shared his story through speaking engagements, radio interviews and magazine articles.

Rob lives in Northern California. Visit his website at afterthefirepress.com.

ALSO BY ROBERT HENSLIN

"Neutrophil's Guide To Stem Cell Transplants for Kids"

A handbook to help guide kids ages 9-12 and their caregivers through stem cell transplants

Full Color Paperback

"Natural Selections, A Collection of 79 Halfway Decent Amateur Photographs"

Photography and Travel Memoir

Full Color Paperback

"When You See the Cows, Make A Left!"

Personal Memoir

Paperback or Kindle eBook

"But I Was in Such a Good Mood This Morning!"

Personal Memoir

Paperback or Kindle eBook

All books are available at Amazon.com.

www.ingramcontent.com/pod-product-compliance
Lightning Source LLC
Chambersburg PA
CBHW071513040426
42444CB00008B/1630